The Playboy of the
Western World
and
Riders to the Sea

Crofts Classics

GENERAL EDITOR

Samuel H. Beer, *Harvard University*

JOHN MILLINGTON SYNGE

The Playboy of the Western World

and

Riders to the Sea

EDITED BY

William E. Hart, M.S.

SAINT JOSEPH COLLEGE
WEST HARTFORD, CONNECTICUT

Harlan Davidson, Inc.
Wheeling, Illinois 60090-6000

Except as permitted under United States copyright law, no part of this
publication may be reproduced or distributed in any form or by any means,
or stored in a database or any retrieval system, without prior written
permission of the publisher. Address inquiries to Harlan Davidson, Inc., 773
Glenn Avenue, Wheeling, Illinois, 60090-6000.

Library of Congress Cataloging-in-Publication Data

Synge, J. M. (John Millington), 1871–1909.
   The playboy of the western world and Riders to the sea.
   (Crofts classics)
   Bibilography: p. 101
   I. Hart, William E. (William Edward). 1929–1987   II. Synge, J. M. (John
Millington), 1871–1909. Riders to the sea. 1986. III. Title. [PR5531.P55
1986]   822'.912   86–8957
ISBN 0-88295-097-5 (pbk.)

Manufactured in the United States of America
00 21 MG

CONTENTS

PRINCIPAL DATES IN THE LIFE OF J. M. SYNGE

❦

1871   16 April. J. M. Synge is born at Newtown Villas, Rathfarnham, a Dublin suburb; he is one of five children of Dublin barrister John Hatch Synge and Kathleen Traill, staunch Evangelical and Low Church.

1872   John Hatch Synge dies. J. M. Synge is raised by his mother and educated in private schools and at home.

1888-1892   Synge studies languages at Trinity College, Dublin, receives B.A., Second Class, takes prizes in Irish and Hebrew, and is awarded Scholarship in counterpoint by Royal Irish Academy of Music.

1893-1898   July. Synge leaves to study music in Germany but soon gives it up for study of languages and literature at Sorbonne. He spends spring or summer near Dublin, passes four months in Italy and in 1896 returns to Paris depressed at Cherry Matheson's refusal to marry him.

1896   December. Synge meets Yeats in Paris.

1897   Synge is operated on for Hodgkins Disease.

1898   February. Synge attends lectures in Celtic Studies at the Sorbonne.
        May-June. He visits the Aran Islands and returns there each summer until 1902.

1898-1902   Synge divides time between Aran and Paris. He writes essays and reviews for various newspapers.

1902   Synge takes active part in the Irish National Theatre Society and during the summer writes *Riders to the Sea* and *The Shadow of the Glen.*

1903   8 October. *The Shadow of the Glen* is first produced.

1904   25 February. *Riders to the Sea* is produced. Abbey Theatre, founded with the generous financial help of Miss A. E. Horniman, opens on December 27th.

1905   4 February. First production of *The Well of the Saints*.

June-July. Synge travels through the Congested Districts with Jack B. Yeats, then visits Kerry and the Blasket Islands alone. Synge, Lady Gregory, and Yeats become directors of the Abbey Theatre. Dissent arises among the actors and several resign.

1906   Synge in love with actress Molly Allgood (Maire O'Neill), and he becomes engaged to her.

1907   26 January. *The Playboy of the Western World* has its first production. There are riots at the Abbey. *The Aran Islands* is published.

1908   Willie and Frank Fay leave the Abbey. Synge is operated on again for Hodgkins Disease; it is impossible to remove tumor.

1909   24 March. Synge dies in Dublin hospital.

11 November. *The Tinker's Wedding* is first produced.

1910   13 January. *Deirdre of the Sorrows* is produced. Synge's *Collected Works* is published in four volumes.

INTRODUCTION

❧

The Background of the Play. Standing like three stone fortresses guarding the mouth of Galway Bay from the fury of the open Atlantic are the Aran Islands. On the middle island, Inishmaan, in the early summer of 1898, J. M. Synge heard the story "about a Connaught man who killed his father with the blow of a spade when he was in passion," and then fled to Inishmaan where, despite police and bounty, the islanders hid him until he escaped to America. This well-known story, recorded by Synge in *The Aran Islands*, provided him not only with the prototype of the Playboy but also with the wild fantasy of a primitive community protecting a criminal from the law.

Through at least five titles, ten complete drafts and a score of scenarios, Synge reworked the material of that Inishmaan story for seven years. As with every play he wrote, it was a long process of acute observation, careful selection, and sensitive creation. Scenes were sketched and abandoned; characters grew in stature and importance, changed names and roles, and often in the interest of theme and design were completely discarded. Among the manuscripts found after Synge's death were seven complete versions of Act I, eight of Act II, and ten of Act III. These manuscripts reveal the playwright's great concern for the orchestral harmony of word, image, mood, rhythm, and gesture in the total design of the play. They also show that the dramatic structure Synge sought to create was less like a regular development to a crisis followed by a resolution than an irregular movement of changing

ix

moods in a work which still maintained its organic unity.[1]

To appreciate better both the way in which Synge refashioned the Inishmaan story and the aesthetics of his astonishing craftsmanship, three principles of his literary criticism must be cited. Not everyone, perhaps not most, will agree with his ideas, but for an understanding of his work it is necessary to know his guiding principles. There is no systematic theory, but at various times and places he gave expression to these principles.

1. "All art is a collaboration."
2. "The drama, like the symphony, does not teach or prove anything."
3. "No personal originality is enough to make a rich work unique, unless it has also the characteristic of a particular time and locality and the life that is in it."

Although in theory the principles are three, actually they are one, for by collaboration Synge meant the artist's attempt to fuse fancy and fact, to wed reality to the ideal, to combine a criticism of things as they are with an aspiration toward things as they can be. He sought to present reality by going to a given people in a given time and place for the subject matter, living speech, psychic moods, attitudes, and emotions of a drama whose purpose was to excite the imagination, relax tensions, and free the spirit.

Thus Synge took as his starting point a primitive community's readiness to hide a criminal who had killed his father with a blow of a spade. This he fashioned into the story of Christy Mahon, a lonely, weak-willed Kerry farm boy who on a dark evening in autumn comes upon an isolated public house along a

[1] For this information I am indebted to Dr. Ann Saddlemyer, Oxford University Press editor of Synge's *Plays, Collected Works,* and associate professor of English at the University of Victoria, British Columbia.

wild coast of Mayo and admits to being on the run
eleven days for having, as he thought, killed his father
with "a blow on the ridge of his skull, laid him
stretched out, and he split to the knob of his gullet."
For what the natives, according to Synge, regard as
the courage and passion of his deed, Christy is hailed
a hero and a marvel. The men fear him; the publican's
lively daughter Pegeen Mike rejects her fiancé Shawn
Keogh for him; the lonely Widow Quin desires him;
the young girls go wild over him, and to be rid of him
Shawn offers him "The half of a ticket to the Western
States!" Under the admiration of the Mayo folk Christy
blossoms from the shy, lonely "loony of Mahon's" to
the champion playboy of the West. Then at the moment of Christy's supreme triumph in sports, in love,
and in poetic speech, his father appears on the scene
very much alive, revealing Christy to be nothing but a
garrulous impostor and destroying his Mayo status as
poet and champion. Yet with an even greater irony,
that same reversal helps to transform Christy into the
very poet and champion the people first considered
him, but now they want no part of him. Praise a boy
and he will prosper, says an Irish proverb. Christy is
praised and he does prosper but not without some
tragic consequence as the play's romantic and Rabelaisian notes come to a climax in this thoroughly Irish
comedy.

As Ireland was always Connaught to Yeats's imagination, so Connaught was always Mayo to Synge's. If
there was a particular Irish time and locality with a
psychic state rich enough to make *The Playboy* dramatically viable and imaginatively acceptable, it was late
19th-century Mayo. As his notebooks and essays on the
Congested Districts reveal, Synge knew Connaught
well, and from this knowledge he drew much of folk
character, mood, incident, imagination, and expression
to collaborate with the life of Mayo, that lonely desolate land of the West "that the Lord created last."
Here nature and history conspired to form "a half-

savage temperament" of traditional rebellion—a temperament made melancholy by the dank weather and desolate isolation, brutalized by the violence of cruel evictions and the Land Wars (1879-1882), restrained at times by faith, anesthetized with poteen, and aroused by any stranger with a wild song or story.

The "particular time" of *The Playboy* is late 19th century Ireland. The "characteristic" of that time is violence bred of earlier famine and fever—a violence engendered by Moonlighters, Agrarian Reform, Land Wars, hanging judges and venal juries, evictions, land grabbing, the Boer War and the "loosèd kharki cutthroats."

The "particular locality" is the isolated district of Ballycroy along the road from Bangor to Malaranny on the North-West coast of Mayo. "Characteristic" of that locality is the wild remoteness to which Synge gives lyric expression not only in his nature descriptions but also in his presentation of the natives' belief that they are a race beyond the ridge of the world.

Synge makes the life of the place itself—"the life that is in it"—a life of drunken talk about violence, brutality, wars, drink, and the grotesqueries of death, hangings, skulls, and a dead man's bones. It is a life whose harsh drudgery is broken by fairs, sports, wakes and weddings; a life whose wild loneliness is forgotten in the thrill of poteen-making, poaching, and the fantasy of the walking dead. It is a life whose spirit is so scarred with the memory of "the treachery of law" and the ordinary violence of "a common week-day kind of murderer" that the coming of a lad with a marvelous tale of fantastic crime and fierce passion is enough to excite the starved imagination of an entire countryside to an equally fantastic exaltation of a father-slayer. The "characteristic of the life in it" is the wildness and unpredictability of the Irish peasantry and their common need to escape the harsh realities, to "have peace now for our drinks."

The Language. To that realistically conceived and artistically controlled setting Synge added the distinction of his dramatic speech founded on Western Ireland's Anglo-Irish dialect. This was the dialect used by persons accustomed to speaking Gaelic who when speaking English still thought in Gaelic, literally translating Irish idioms into English expressions. Thus Anglo-Irish takes most of its vocabulary from English, but its habit of thought and idiom come from Irish.

Synge's Anglo-Irish dialect is distinctive for its Irish imagery in descriptions of nature and love and for its lilting rhythms. What Synge did with that dialect was to fashion it into a dramatically functional poetic speech that defines, intensifies, and extends setting, character, and action. Although his language has often been attacked as too violent and too ornate, and too artificial in its striving for rhythm, it cannot be denied that there is in his speech a fundamental realism, a living quality that is highly effective. As an illustration of this, read aloud the opening lines of the play, the famous love scene in Act III, and Christy's fiery speeches toward the end of the play. Synge's dialogue may have its limitations, but it should be considered that, except for comic relief, dialect had rarely been used in the English theatre; Synge and his fellow Abbey dramatists proved that the Irish peasantry and their habits of speech could be the substance and the medium of sublime tragedy and fine comedy.

Synge's language is not difficult. In *The Playboy* there are only about twelve words of strictly Irish origin; the relatively few archaic or Tudor forms of English words that appear are easily understood. Some of the more common Anglo-Irish constructions in the play are the following: the pleonastic infinitive form **for to** in place of the usual English **to**: "Six yards of stuff **for to** make a yellow gown"; the use of **after** with a form of the verb **to be** to express an action just completed: "**Aren't** we **after** making a good bargain"; the use of **and** in place of such conjunctions as **when, while, since, although** to introduce various subordinate clauses: "How would you see him **and** it dark night this half hour gone by"; "he'll be having my life, **and** I going home"; a marked preference for using the present participle with the infinitive **to be,** and the use of **do be** to express habit or frequency: "It was a dark lonesome place **to be hearing** the like of him"; "Is it often the polis **do be coming** into this place, master of the house?" Other Anglo-Irish expressions which Synge frequently uses are **the way** to indicate result, **the way** and **what way** to mean **how** or **why,** and **in it** to mean **present:** "Aren't we after making a good bargain, **the way** we're only waiting these days"; "And **what way** weren't you hanged, mister?"; "There'd be no harm staying now, I'm thinking, and himself **in it** too." Another peculiarity is the use of **itself** meaning **even:** "If you're a dunce **itself,** you'd have a right to know . . ."

Synge and Irish Humor. Synge's humor in its matter and manner is thoroughly Irish. Like the medieval bards and the poets of the 17th and 18th centuries Synge used the common subjects of popular humor: the "made match" that wed May to December and haggled over the size of dowries, the clergy, the self-glorification over the saints of the race, and the people's tendency to lose themselves in imagination, blinding themselves to actuality. Especially in these two latter objects of comedy Synge anticipates the work of Joyce, O'Casey, O'Flaherty, O'Connor, and Behan. The Irish quality of Synge's humor is evidenced in such scenes as the girls idolizing Christy, Christy biting Shawn, and Pegeen burning Christy in retaliation. Irish is the macabre and grotesque humor, born of the peasants' ambivalent attitude toward life and death, expressed in the drunken riot attending Kate Cassidy's wake and by the men "stretched out retching speechless on the holy stones." Again macabre and grotesque is the talk of skulls "ranged out like blue jugs in a cabin of Connaught" and Philly's remark about the graveyard "remnants of a man who had thighs as long as your arm" which he would put together "for fun" many a fine Sunday. Typical of Irish humor is the verbal irony of such passages as "Marcus Quin, God rest him, got six months for maiming ewes, and he a great warrant [with a great gift] to tell stories of holy Ireland" and Christy's reply to the question did he kill his father: "With the help of God I did surely, and that the Holy Immaculate Mother may intercede for his soul." Perhaps what is most Irish in Synge's humor is the comic practice of developing to an extreme point the implications of a situation so that no aspect of life is too sacred to be spared the mockery of laughter. It is the atavistic play-spirit, a regression to the pagan half-belief that refuses to take either mortals or immortals too seriously. In the play nothing escapes this humor—neither life nor death, God nor the Angels, saints nor devils, prophets nor Pope, Cardinals nor priests, neither "the preaching north" nor the Erris plain, romance nor hatred, neither the intrigue of poaching nor the escape of poteen.

The personal distinction of Synge's humor is his irony. It is an attitude of half-cynical factitious hope born of his own lonely agnostic vision. He thought sardonic laughter the healthy attitude for one convinced that the only resolution of life's problem is the grave "with worms eternally." Yeats referred to this skeptical attitude when he wrote of "the astringent joy and hardness" in all Synge did. Again it was Synge's ironic view of life Yeats spoke of when he said that "the strength that made him delight in setting the hard virtues by the soft, the bitter by the sweet, salt by mercury, the stone by the elixir, gave him a hunger for harsh facts, for ugly surprising things, for all that defies our hope." In *The Playboy* irony is everywhere: in the title which may be freely rendered "The World's Champion Impostor," and in the plot as illusion creates a hero from an awkward boy while reality, destroying the illusion, makes him an even greater hero. In the play's portrayal of every man's need to be a hero, if only to himself, and everyone's need to have a hero, if only for sacrifice, here again is the frozen laugh at the folly of men.

Riot in the Abbey Theatre. Originally the play was scheduled to open in early December. Synge, however, had trouble completing the third act, and *The Playboy* did not have its premiere until January 26, 1907. It was a Synge program and, as scheduled, played for seven nights. *Riders to the Sea,* an established favorite with Dublin audiences, opened the program. *The Playboy* followed and roused the audience to such a pitch of resentment that their vexed spirit erupted in shouts of anger. Trouble over *The Playboy* had been anticipated. In Dublin, before the play went into rehearsal, it was read to Lady Gregory and Yeats who complained that there was far too much bad language and too many violent oaths. Willie Fay, an actor sensitive to audience response and fearful of the play's effect, begged Synge to make a few changes. The changes would not have amounted to five percent of the play, but Synge refused. Though he did not intend to slander Ireland or to ridicule the people of the West, Synge did mean to annoy and shock his Dublin audience. In his opinion, between the Irish peasants and the Irish men of genius there stood "an ungodly ruck of fat faced, sweaty headed, swine"—just the kind of people who had rejected *The Well of the Saints,* taking offence where none had been intended. Whether or not one is willing to accept Willie Fay's word that Synge admitted an intended attack upon his audience, whether or not one gives credence to a critic's word "that at its first performance Christy Mahon was played by W. G. Fay as a moral degenerate, by the express directions of the author," it cannot be denied that there was much in *The Playboy* to offend an Irish audience. No artist can afford to disregard the attitudes of his audience, and if he does, he has to pay the price. Synge was unwise not to accept the advice of his friends and fellow dramatists, for although he knew Western Ireland better than they, they knew Dublin better than he did.

Thus when the first act went off well, Lady Gregory hastened to wire "play great success" to Yeats who was lecturing in Scotland. Her judgment was premature. At the close of the third act another telegram was sent to Yeats, saying: "Audience broke up in disorder at the word shift."

The question may reasonably be asked, was the word "shift" the cause of the uproar or did it merely mark the point where the audience's emotions became explosive? It is hard to see why a word so commonly used in ordinary conversation to signify a woman's slip or chemise should create such an uproar in this instance. The Anglophile element, however, seized upon it and ridiculed the Irish as if they were exceedingly prudish or unreasonably sensitive about the purity of Irish women. Whether the aim was conscious or unconscious this merely served to cover over the very real causes of Irish resentment. The resentment had been building throughout the play until it found violent expression at that fatal line where Christy protested that he would not give up Pegeen, not even if all the girls in Ireland were offered to him—no, not even if they stood before him half dressed.

Any fair-minded person can see why the Irish should resent the play. First of all, it was an affront to their national pride. There is not a noble character in the play. The men are either drunken boors or knaves. The women are something less than respectable. It is within the legitimate function of the comedy writer in his role as censor of morals to mock the foibles of men and institutions, but Synge went unpardonably far. His was not acceptable comedy; his was a bitter lampoon. About one hundred and twenty-five years earlier another Irishman, Edmund Burke, said that he did not know how to draw up an indictment against an entire people, but this is what Synge, in effect, did. If there had been one villain or two villains the Irish would not have complained, but when every character in the play was undeserving of respect, the Irish audience could have said: "Is this Mayo? Is this Ireland?" Their violent response was only natural.

In addition to this, Synge needlessly affronted the Catholic religion of the Irish. Many of the Irish may have been lax in observing their religion, but they did not intend to permit an outsider to ridicule it. Although the peasants' readiness to use sacred names and popular religious expressions does lend itself at times to unintended humor, the dramatist's frequent and irreverent use of such names and expressions prompted even his close friends, Yeats and Lady Gregory, to object.

Lastly, the play was regarded as injurious to the rising cause of Nationalism. For years the Irish had been struggling for some measure of self-government. Throughout the land there were societies, clubs, leagues—some of them demanding Home Rule, some demanding complete independence from England, some advocating violent measures, others, the orderly process of the law, but all of them recognizing the need of world sympathy and esteem if their aims were to be successful. If the Irish were as low and as sordid as the play portrayed them, what chance was there of gaining the goodwill of the world? The play therefore was bitterly resented as one more obstacle in the way of that freedom for which the Irish were so earnestly, so impatiently struggling. There were Irishmen who wanted, and wrongly so, to make the theatre a propaganda instrument to advance their political claims. Others would have been content if the theatre had remained neutral, but most Irishmen bitterly resented the fact that the theatre movement, born to banish the stage Irishman and to promote what was best in the race, should present the tragic reality of the Congested Districts[2] in a dispassionate, comic, and distorted way that would supply gratuitous arguments to the enemies of Ireland. Synge and his fellow dramatists may not have understood or attached any importance to these considerations, but that was either their misfortune or their fault.

With the final curtain of that first Saturday night the word went forth to pub, press, and priest that Synge had done it again. That same Abbey playwright who four years earlier had attacked the honor of Irish womanhood with his portrait of Nora Burke in *The Shadow of the Glen* had now vilified Ireland again. A battle royal was in the making. By Monday night the greatest uproar in the history of the Abbey Theatre had begun. The tumult lasted a week. Riot in the pit, dumb show on the stage, police in the aisles, chant of "The Peeler and the Goat," shouts of "God save the King," arrests in the theatre, and fines in the courts— that was the Dublin reaction to *The Playboy*. Yeats rushed home from Scotland to direct the attack against "mob censorship." Not until Saturday night, February 2nd, did the play enjoy an uninterrupted performance, but the damage had been done. Everything about the play—its construction, its taste, its fundamental idea— was venomously criticized. The wild use of holy names and religious allusions, the characteristic comic ir-reverence of rural folk, suddenly became blasphemy. The unusual amount of bad language and the fact that Pegeen was left alone under the same roof for the whole night with Christy and quite unchaperoned (she didn't lock the door) was a gross and wanton insult to Irish womanhood, but that Irish maidens

[2] **Congested Districts:** poverty stricken areas of Connaught, es-pecially along the coast of Mayo and Connemara. Synge wrote a number of articles on these areas for *The Manchester Guardian* and later published them under the title of *The Congested Dis-tricts*. The government had set up a board by the same name to help cope with the situation.

should ever be thought of as "a drift [a herd] of chosen females standing in their shifts" or that an Irish community would ever fall at the feet of an avowed father-slayer was calumny carried to extremes.

Riot in the Press. From the Abbey the riot spread to the newspapers. Judgments were formed according to the basic policies of each paper; Nationalist press condemned, and Anglo press defended the play. While *The Freeman's Journal* raged that *The Playboy* was a vicious satire, an "unmitigated, protracted libel upon Irish peasant men and . . . Irish peasant girlhood," and while *The Dublin Evening Telegraph* bitterly complained that "the hideous caricature would be slanderous of a Kaffir krall," *The Irish Times* fired back that it was a most accurate representation of Irish life, a "highly moral play, deriving its motives from sources as pure and as lofty as the externals of its setting are necessarily wild and vulgar." Press-heated arguments, pro and con, had the result of obscuring the essential import of the play. Synge himself helped to complicate the problem of the play's meaning when, in an interview with an *Evening Mail* reporter immediately after the second night's performance, he implied that the work was not to be taken seriously by claiming that *The Playboy* was "an extravaganza, made to amuse." Though he retracted the comment two days later in a letter to *The Irish Times,* the opinion had already gone forth. George A. Birmingham (Rev. J. O. Hannay) repeated the "comic extravaganza" theory in *The Morning Leader.* On Wednesday London's *Times* reported "extravaganza with a motive," further noting that to many the play was "a legitimate *reductio ad absurdum* of the tendencies of peasant life in the remote west of Ireland."

Though the play ran for only one week, the controversy over its meaning and interpretation raged on. By spring critics had begun to view Shawn Keogh as an example of what emigration was doing to Ireland, leaving the country with the lunatic fringe and nothing but the unfittest of the unfit to continue the race. By June Lady Gregory had broadened the critics' view of Shawn to encompass the whole play when, at *The Playboy's* London premiere in the Great Queen Street Theatre, she suggested "that the play may be taken as a prophecy of what Irish peasant life will be like when emigration has robbed Ireland of all men of character and daring." Thus did friend and foe alike complicate the significance of the play.

The controversial opinions that echoed in the press in those first few months gave rise to subsequent explanations by later critics, conflicting in their interpretations, and their various views in turn were to perplex future producers and actors for whom the Abbey riots would be not a memory but a factual footnote in the history of world theatre. They would ask how the play was to be interpreted. Was it to be regarded as a political satire?—As symbolism with some recondite meaning?—As extravaganza? Was it to be given a straightforward interpretation according to the meaning of the words? Now, a half-century removed from the controversies of 1907, the traditional *Playboy* criticism of mordant satire, hard core realism, and extravaganza appears to owe more to the riots in the theatre and the press than to an objective reading of the play itself. In its short history it has been produced according to all these various interpretations, but always with something to be desired. Little, however, was left to be desired at the play's London premiere of 1907.

As it was natural for *The Playboy* to excite riots in Dublin, it was natural for it to be acclaimed in London. The English could be as dispassionate about the work as the Irish had been impassioned by it precisely because there was very little in the play to offend the religious, political, or national sensibilities of an English audience. To the artist and his work the honest tribute of enthusiastic admiration so fiercely denied along the Liffey was heartily given along the Thames. For a happy while Synge was the toast of London. Eventually the controversies in Ireland died out, but the criticism they had voiced continued to hound *The Playboy* like Old Mahon himself so that with one voice Christy and the play could shout: "Where'll I hide my poor body from that ghost of hell?"

Humor, Propaganda, Art. Willie Fay had cautioned Synge that if he attacked his audience he had to expect the audience to retaliate. Too much anger on the stage, Willie said, creates anger in the audience. When the riots had passed, writers like Padraic Colum, George Moore, and George Russell were inclined to agree with Fay; they felt that the excess of violence and realism of the last act had triggered the riots. Synge's reaction, however, was to say that Irish humor was dead. That complaint was characteristic of his own politically disinterested artistic temperament, and in a very real yet limited sense Synge was right. No oppressed people can laugh at their own abject conditions, the practical philosophy of the sardonic laugh is no healthy solution to oppression. Synge realized that a riotous humor could be distilled from the Westerner's irresponsible spirit which he so much admired. Synge realized too that the wild laughter and the bitter tears at the heart of the Connaught temperament were in large measure the tragic result of the cruel oppression practiced by his own Ascendancy class. Nevertheless, in his drama he was too stubborn and too determined an artist ever to soften the irony of his vision on account of the ensuing tear. Thus it was inevitable that where he sought honestly to stir gypsy laughter he fanned the fires of hidden anger. His comedy was tragic. It was his sad fate to be writing for audiences who were not in the mood for the subtle counterpointing of reality and illusion, of the romantic and Rabelaisian, of the lyric and ironic. As Yeats had said, Synge's Ireland was not the place for a dramatist with "an intense, narrow personality," not the climate for a genius with a "harsh, independent, heroical, clean, wind-swept view of things."

Nevertheless Yeats was determined to improve the climate. He knew Synge's work would provoke an attack; he welcomed and promoted *The Playboy* uproar. The time had come to do battle with all those who would deny Irish writers what he called "the freedom to find in their own land every expression of good and evil necessary to their art." Thus for Yeats and Lady Gregory *The Playboy* battle became a fight against what she called "mob censorship" and what Yeats referred to as the theatre's quarrel with "the old Puritanism, the old dislike of power and reality." So intense were Yeats's feelings for Synge and the freedom of Irish writers that he regarded the enemies of *The Playboy* as men whose hatred would sterilize the native imagination and emasculate the native genius necessary to the rebirth of a national literature. Thus, in prose and poetry, Yeats likened the play's enemies to eunuchs running through Hell screeching to catch a glimpse of Don Juan riding by.

An Enigma to the Critics. The history of *The Playboy* criticism bears adequate testimony to the fact that actors, producers, and critics have found the play to be something of a problem in meaning and interpretation. Actors have found fault with the play's resolution. Producers have foundered over the dilemma of whether the play is essentially realistic or fantastic, and critics have compounded the problem by ascribing to the work themes often contradictory and sometimes freakish. Critics have placed the play in so many different classifications that one is reminded of Polonius' description in *Hamlet* of the repertoire of the players who came to Elsinore. Critics have run amuck, one or another of them saying that the play is extravaganza, free comedy, Dionysiac comedy, comic pastoral, historic pastoral, mock pastoral, tragic history, satire, tragi-comedy, and tragedy. Such labels are of importance only to the critics. Synge called his play "A Comedy in Three Acts." For us that should be enough. Beyond that, for the problem of meaning itself, all one can do is to suggest that the problem derives both from the complexity of the work and from the author's general denial of the intention of pointing a lesson or proving a thesis in his dramatic works. Thus every reader, every actor, is left to experience the play and to draw his own conclusions from the action and situations described.

THE IRISH DRAMATIC MOVEMENT

The last phase of the nationalistic movement which swept Ireland in the late 19th century was the Irish Literary Revival. Born of that revival was the Irish Dramatic Movement. W. B. Yeats became its first high priest and the Abbey Theatre its temple. In 1891, at the age of twenty-six, the young poet began his priesthood in London with the founding of the Irish Literary Society. In Dublin the following year he founded the National Literary Society to promote the study of Irish literature, music, and art. Between that time and the founding of the Irish Literary Theatre in 1899 Yeats gathered about himself kindred spirits in the persons of Edward Martyn, Lady Gregory, and George Moore. With them he discussed the possibility of founding a small theatre to bring to the stage the deeper thoughts and emotions of the Irish and to "show that Ireland is not the home of buffoonery and of easy sentiment, as it has been represented, but the home of an ancient idealism."

Before the close of the century the movement had both Irish plays and playwrights, but it did not have a complete company of Irish players until Yeats' discovery in 1901 of a group of part-time, amateur actors,

Dublin clerks and shop girls, led by the two amateur producers and brilliant actors William and Frank Fay. In 1902 A. E. (George Russell) and J. M. Synge began to take an active part in the theatre movement which by then had come under the new title of the Irish National Theatre Society. The first performances given by the Society were Yeats' *Cathleen ni Houlihan* and A.E.'s *Deirdre* produced at St. Teresa's Hall, Dublin, in April, 1902. A brief visit to London in May of 1903 enchanted English reviewers with the refreshing simplicity, beautiful speech, and natural acting of the Irish players. That London success attracted the attention and interest of an English woman by the name of Miss A. E. F. Horniman. With her financial assistance in 1904 the Society of Irish plays, players, and playwrights found a permanent home on Lower Abbey Street, Dublin. Two adjacent buildings, one The People's Music Hall of the Mechanics' Institute and the other an old morgue, were converted into an auditorium 42 feet wide and 51 feet deep with a pockethandkerchief stage 15 feet deep, 21 feet wide and 14 feet high at the proscenium arch, a seating capacity of 562, a remarkable talent for developing great players and dramatists, and an unholy habit of rejecting with stormy riots the very genius it cradled. Within a decade the achievement of the Abbey was so formidable that the theatre world was astonished to admiration and imitation in seeing so much genius take fire in so short a time and from so small a place.

Much of the credit for the Abbey's accomplishment belongs to Yeats, Lady Gregory, Synge, and the Fays. It is a too artificial and inaccurate summation to say that Yeats was the theorist, Lady Gregory the business manager, and Synge the supreme artist, for all three of them were playwrights. Yet, were it not for their individual talent, their art alone would not have sufficed to sustain the theatre movement. In them, courage, ideals, purpose, and patriotism combined to reject realism and the Ibsenite problem play, the English theatre's commercialism, and the pseudo-patriotism of fanatic Philistines in pulpit and press.

To the theatre Yeats gave life and direction. Through the poetic dramatization of Ireland's saga literature and living folklore, Yeats proposed to show Ireland's native genius and imagination and by doing so, in the workshop experience of theatre aided by language and imagination, create a new national literature that would raise the dignity of Ireland. He did it. He called the drama back to the sovereignty of words. He fashioned a people's theatre by reforming a popular theatre to receive plays that were part of the living imagination of the people. The warrior king fighting the waves and the potato poet wielding a spade, the woman with "the walk of a Queen" and the tramp in the lonely glen—each had a place in the Abbey. Yeats reformed a theatre and educated common people to enjoy with the simplicity of the understanding heart what scholars could create by the disciplined effort of the working mind. By rejecting the then popular mass of stage conventions with all the purposeless gesturing and irrelevant movement by insisting on the subordination of action and scenery to the words with their musical intonation and emotional intensity, Yeats made his theatre a place alive with intellectual excitement. Natural acting, clear delivery, and simple settings with nothing distracting to break the spell—this was Yeats's principle that became the hallmark of an Abbey production.

Although the Irish Dramatic Movement served admirably to call the English theatre back to the poetic drama, the Irish theatre itself after Synge gave up some of its poetic character for the more realistic and naturalistic drama of Robinson, Murray, O'Casey, and Carroll. It remains to be seen whether the new Abbey rising phoenix-like from the fire that destroyed it in 1951 shall continue to be for Ireland a theatre "with a base of realism and an apex of beauty."

THE PLAYBOY OF THE WESTERN WORLD

A Comedy in Three Acts

THE PLAYBOY OF THE WESTERN WORLD

PREFACE

In writing THE PLAYBOY OF THE WESTERN WORLD, as in my other plays, I have used one or two words only that I have not heard among the country people of Ireland, or spoken in my own nursery before I could read the newspapers. A certain number of the phrases I employ I have heard also from herds and fishermen along the coast from Kerry to Mayo, or from beggar-women and ballad-singers nearer Dublin; and I am glad to acknowledge how much I owe to the folk-imagination of these fine people. Anyone who has lived in real intimacy with the Irish peasantry will know that the wildest sayings and ideas in this play are tame indeed, compared with the fancies one may hear in any little hillside cabin in Geesala, or Carraroe, or Dingle Bay. All art is a collaboration; and there is little doubt that in the happy ages of literature, striking and beautiful phrases were as ready to the story-teller's or the playwright's hand, as the rich cloaks and dresses of his time. It is probable that when the Elizabethan dramatist took his ink-horn and sat down to his work he used many phrases that he had just heard, as he sat at dinner, from his mother or his children. In Ireland, those of us who know the people have the same privilege. When I was writing *The Shadow of the Glen*, some years ago, I got more aid than any learning could have given me from a chink in the floor of the old Wicklow house where I was staying, that let me hear what was being said by the servant girls in the kitchen. This matter, I think, is of importance, for in countries where the imagination of the people, and the language they use, is rich and living, it is possible for a writer to be rich and copious in his words, and at the same time to give the reality, which is the root of all poetry, in a comprehensive and natural form. In the modern literature of towns, however, richness is found only in sonnets, or prose poems, or in one or two elaborate books that are far away from the profound and common interests of life. One has, on one side, Mallarmé and Huysmans producing this literature; and on the other, Ibsen and Zola dealing with the reality of life in joyless and pallid words. On the stage one must have reality, and one must have joy; and that is why the intellectual modern drama has failed, and people have grown sick of the false joy of the musical comedy, that has been given them in place of the rich joy found only in what is superb and wild in reality. In a good play every speech should be as fully flavoured as a nut or apple, and such speeches cannot be written by anyone who works among people who have shut their lips on poetry. In Ireland, for a few years more, we have a popular imagination that is fiery and magnificent, and tender; so that those of us who wish to write start with a chance that is not given to writers in places where the springtime of the local life has been forgotten, and the harvest is a memory only, and the straw has been turned into bricks.

J.M.S.

January 21st, 1907.

THE PLAYBOY OF THE WESTERN WORLD

PERSONS

CHRISTOPHER MAHON

OLD MAHON, *his father, a squatter*

MICHAEL JAMES FLAHERTY (*called* MICHAEL JAMES), *a publican*

MARGARET FLAHERTY (*called* PEGEEN MIKE), *his daughter*

WIDOW QUIN, *a woman of about thirty*

SHAWN KEOGH, *her* [*second*] *cousin, a young farmer*

PHILLY CULLEN *and* JIMMY FARRELL, *small farmers*[1]

SARA TANSEY, SUSAN BRADY *and* HONOR BLAKE [*and* NELLY], *village girls*

A BELLMAN

SOME PEASANTS

The action takes place near a village, on a wild coast of Mayo. The First Act passes on an evening of autumn, the other two Acts on the following day.

---

[1] **small farmers** poor farmers

THE PLAYBOY OF THE WESTERN WORLD

Act I

SCENE: *Country public house or shebeen, very rough and untidy. There is a sort of counter on the right with shelves, holding many bottles and jugs, just seen above it. Empty barrels stand near the counter. At back, a little to left of counter, there is a door into the open air, then, more to the left, there is a settle with shelves above it, with more jugs, and a table beneath a window. At the left there is a large open fireplace, with turf fire, and a small door into inner room.* PEGEEN, *a wild-looking but fine girl, of about twenty, is writing at table. She is dressed in the usual peasant dress.*

PEGEEN (*slowly as she writes*). Six yards of stuff for to make a yellow gown. A pair of lace boots with lengthy heels on them and brassy eyes. A hat is suited for a wedding day. A fine tooth comb. To be sent with three barrels of porter in Jimmy Farrell's creel cart[1] on the evening of the coming Fair[2] to Mister Michael James Flaherty. With the best compliments of this season. Margaret Flaherty.

SHAWN KEOGH (*a fat and fair young man comes in as she signs, looks round awkwardly, when he sees she is alone*). Where's himself?[3]

PEGEEN (*without looking at him*). He's coming. (*She*

---

[1] **creel cart** cart with open, barred, or grated sides used to carry turf, sheep, pigs, etc. [2] **Fair** the high day for talk and commerce in livestock, held in the middle of the month [3] **himself** the master of the house, Michael James

directs letter.) To Mister Sheamus Mulroy, Wine and
Spirit Dealer, Castlebar.[4]

SHAWN (*uneasily*). I didn't see him on the road.

PEGEEN. How would you see him (*licks stamp and
puts it on letter*) and it dark night this half hour gone
by?

SHAWN (*turning towards door again*). I stood a
while outside wondering would I have a right to pass
on or to walk in and see you, Pegeen Mike (*comes to
fire*), and I could hear the cows breathing, and sighing
in the stillness of the air, and not a step moving any
place from this gate to the bridge.

PEGEEN (*putting letter in envelope*). It's above at
the cross-roads he is meeting Philly Cullen; and a
couple more are going along with him to Kate Cassidy's wake.[5]

SHAWN (*looking at her blankly*). And he's going
that length in the dark night?

PEGEEN (*impatiently*). He is surely, and leaving me
lonesome on the scruff of the hill. (*She gets up and
puts envelope on dresser, then winds clock.*) Isn't it
long the nights are now, Shawn Keogh, to be leaving
a poor girl with her own self counting the hours to the
dawn of day?

SHAWN (*with awkward humour*). If it is, when we're
wedded in a short while you'll have no call[6] to com-
plain, for I've little will to be walking off to wakes or
weddings in the darkness of the night.

PEGEEN (*with rather scornful good humour*). You're
making mighty certain, Shaneen,[7] that I'll wed you
now.

SHAWN. Aren't we after making a good bargain,[8]
the way we're only waiting these days on Father
Reilly's dispensation[9] from the bishops, or the Court
of Rome.

---

[4] **Castlebar** a principal city of East Mayo [5] **wake** the watching
of the dead, once an occasion for riot and drunkenness [6] **no
call** no need [7] **Shaneen** little Shawn [8] **bargain** Shawn's fair
day view of marriage [9] **dispensation** to marry his *second* cousin

PEGEEN (*looking at him teasingly, washing up at dresser*). It's a wonder, Shaneen, the Holy Father'd be taking notice of the likes of you; for if I was him I wouldn't bother with this place where you'll meet none but Red Linahan, has a squint in his eye, and Patcheen is lame in his heel, or the mad Mulrannies were driven from California and they lost in their wits. We're a queer lot these times to go troubling the Holy Father on his sacred seat.

SHAWN (*scandalized*). If we are, we're as good this place as another, maybe, and as good these times as we were for ever.

PEGEEN (*with scorn*). As good, is it? Where now will you meet the like of Daneen Sullivan knocked the eye from a peeler,[10] or Marcus Quin, God rest him, got six months for maiming ewes, and he a great warrant[11] to tell stories of holy Ireland till he'd have the old women shedding down tears about their feet. Where will you find the like of them, I'm saying?

SHAWN (*timidly*). If you don't, it's a good job, maybe; for (*with peculiar emphasis on the words*) Father Reilly has small conceit[12] to have that kind walking around and talking to the girls.

PEGEEN (*impatiently, throwing water from basin out of the door*). Stop tormenting me with Father Reilly (*imitating his voice*) when I'm asking only what way[13] I'll pass these twelve hours of dark, and not take my death with the fear.

(*Looking out of door*)

SHAWN (*timidly*). Would I fetch you the Widow Quin, maybe?

PEGEEN. Is it the like of that murderer? You'll not, surely.

SHAWN (*going to her, soothingly*). Then I'm thinking himself will stop along with you when he sees

[10] **peeler** policeman, so-called after Sir Robert Peel   [11] **a great warrant** a great gift for, a great hand at   [12] **conceit** a liking, a fancy for   [13] **what way** how

you taking on, for it'll be a long night-time with great darkness, and I'm after feeling a kind of fellow above in the furzy ditch, groaning wicked like a maddening dog, the way[14] it's good cause you have, maybe, to be fearing now.

PEGEEN (*turning on him sharply*). What's that? Is it a man you seen?

SHAWN (*retreating*). I couldn't see him at all; but I heard him groaning out, and breaking his heart. It should have been a young man from his words speaking.

PEGEEN (*going after him*). And you never went near to see was he hurted or what ailed him at all?

SHAWN. I did not, Pegeen Mike. It was a dark lonesome place to be hearing the like of him.

PEGEEN. Well, you're a daring fellow, and if they find his corpse stretched above in the dews of dawn, what'll you say then to the peelers, or the Justice of the Peace?

SHAWN (*thunderstruck*). I wasn't thinking of that. For the love of God, Pegeen Mike, don't let on[15] I was speaking of him. Don't tell your father and the men is coming above; for if they heard that story, they'd have great blabbing this night at the wake.

PEGEEN. I'll maybe tell them, and I'll maybe not.

SHAWN. They are coming at the door. Will you whisht,[16] I'm saying?

PEGEEN. Whisht yourself.

(*She goes behind counter.* MICHAEL JAMES, *fat jovial publican, comes in followed by* PHILLY CULLEN, *who is thin and mistrusting, and* JIMMY FARRELL, *who is fat and amorous, about forty-five.*)

MEN (*together*). God bless you. The blessing of God on this place.

PEGEEN. God bless you kindly.[17]

[14] the way so that   [15] let on don't admit   [16] whisht be quiet, shut up   [17] God bless you kindly Irish ritual blessing on entering a house

MICHAEL (*to men who go to the counter*). Sit down now, and take your rest. (*Crosses to* SHAWN *at the fire*) And how is it you are, Shawn Keogh? Are you coming over the sands to Kate Cassidy's wake?

SHAWN. I am not, Michael James. I'm going home the short cut to my bed.

PEGEEN (*speaking across the counter*). He's right too, and have you no shame, Michael James, to be quitting off for the whole night, and leaving myself lonesome in the shop?

MICHAEL (*good-humouredly*). Isn't it the same whether I go for the whole night or a part only? and I'm thinking it's a queer daughter you are if you'd have me crossing backward through the Stooks[18] of the Dead Women, with a drop taken.[19]

PEGEEN. If I am a queer daughter, it's a queer father'd be leaving me lonesome these twelve hours of dark, and I piling the turf with the dogs barking, and the calves mooing, and my own teeth rattling with the fear.

JIMMY (*flatteringly*). What is there to hurt you, and you a fine, hardy girl would knock the head of any two men in the place?

PEGEEN (*working herself up*). Isn't there the harvest boys[20] with their tongues red for drink, and the ten tinkers[21] is camped in the east glen, and the thousand militia[22]—bad cess[23] to them!—walking idle through the land. There's lots surely to hurt me, and I won't stop alone in it, let himself do what he will.

MICHAEL. If you're that afeard,[24] let Shawn Keogh stop along with you. It's the will of God, I'm thinking, himself should be seeing to you now.

[18] **Stooks** rocks or low dunes along the sea-shore, shaped like *stooks,* shocks of corn generally containing 12 sheaves   [19] **drop taken** drunk   [20] **harvest boys** workers who migrated to Scotland and England to help with the harvest and who returned in late autumn with a few pounds to help survive the winter   [21] **tinkers** the gypsies of the Irish roads   [22] **militia** part of the military garrison that once numbered over 35,000 in Ireland and no friend to the people   [23] **bad cess** bad luck   [24] **afeard** afraid

(They all turn on SHAWN.*)*

SHAWN *(in horrified confusion)*. I would and welcome,[25] Michael James, but I'm afeard of Father Reilly; and what at all would the Holy Father and the Cardinals of Rome be saying if they heard I did the like of that?

MICHAEL *(with contempt)*. God help you! Can't you sit in by the hearth with the light lit and herself[26] beyond in the room? You'll do that surely, for I've heard tell there's a queer fellow above, going mad or getting his death, maybe, in the gripe[27] of the ditch, so she'd be safer this night with a person here.

SHAWN *(with plaintive despair)*. I'm afeard of Father Reilly, I'm saying. Let you not be tempting me, and we near married itself.

PHILLY *(with cold contempt)*. Lock him in the west room. He'll stay then and have no sin to be telling to the priest.

MICHAEL *(to* SHAWN, *getting between him and the door)*. Go up now.[28]

SHAWN *(at the top of his voice)*. Don't stop me, Michael James. Let me out of the door, I'm saying, for the love of the Almighty God. Let me out *(trying to dodge past him)*. Let me out of it, and may God grant you His indulgence in the hour of need.

MICHAEL *(loudly)*. Stop your noising, and sit down by the hearth.

(Gives him a push and goes to counter laughing)

SHAWN *(turning back, wringing his hands)*. Oh, Father Reilly and the saints of God, where will I hide myself today? Oh, St. Joseph and St. Patrick and St. Brigid, and St. James, have mercy on me now!

*(*SHAWN *turns round, sees door clear, and makes a rush for it.)*

[25] would and welcome gladly   [26] and herself while Pegeen is
[27] gripe the hollow, the trench   [28] Go up now get back to the hearth

MICHAEL (*catching him by the coat-tail*). You'd be going, is it?

SHAWN (*screaming*). Leave me go, Michael James, leave me go, you old Pagan, leave me go, or I'll get the curse of the priests on you, and of the scarlet-coated bishops of the courts of Rome.

(*With a sudden movement he pulls himself out of his coat, and disappears out of the door, leaving his coat in* MICHAEL'S *hands.*)

MICHAEL (*turning round, and holding up coat*). Well, there's the coat of a Christian man. Oh, there's sainted glory this day in the lonesome west; and by the will of God I've got you a decent man, Pegeen, you'll have no call to be spying after if you've a score of young girls, maybe, weeding in your fields.

PEGEEN (*taking up the defence of her property*). What right have you to be making game of a poor fellow for minding the priest, when it's your own the fault is, not paying a penny pot-boy[29] to stand along with me and give me courage in the doing of my work?

(*She snaps the coat away from him, and goes behind counter with it.*)

MICHAEL (*taken aback*). Where would I get a pot-boy? Would you have me send the bell-man screaming in the streets of Castlebar?

SHAWN (*opening the door a chink and putting in his head, in a small voice*). Michael James!

MICHAEL (*imitating him*). What ails you?

SHAWN. The queer dying fellow's beyond looking over the ditch. He's come up, I'm thinking, stealing your hens. (*Looks over his shoulder*) God help me, he's following me now (*he runs into room*), and if he's heard what I said, he'll be having my life, and I going home lonesome in the darkness of the night.

(*For a perceptible moment they watch the door with curiosity. Someone coughs outside. Then* CHRISTY

[29] **pot-boy** a menial in a public house

MAHON, *a slight young man, comes in very tired and frightened and dirty.*)

CHRISTY (*in a small voice*). God save all here!

MEN. God save you kindly.

CHRISTY (*going to the counter*). I'd trouble you for a glass of porter, woman of the house.

(*He puts down coin.*)

PEGEEN (*serving him*). You're one of the tinkers, young fellow, is beyond camped in the glen?

CHRISTY. I am not; but I'm destroyed walking.

MICHAEL (*patronizingly*). Let you come up then to the fire. You're looking famished with the cold.

CHRISTY. God reward you. (*He takes up his glass and goes a little way across to the left, then stops and looks about him.*) Is it often the polis[30] do be coming into this place, master of the house?

MICHAEL. If you'd come in better hours, you'd have seen "Licensed for the sale of Beer and Spirits, to be consumed on the premises," written in white letters above the door, and what would the polis want spying on me, and not a decent house within four miles, the way every living Christian is a bona fide,[31] saving one widow alone?

CHRISTY (*with relief*). It's a safe house, so.

(*He goes over to the fire, sighing and moaning. Then he sits down putting his glass beside him and begins gnawing a turnip, too miserable to feel the others staring at him with curiosity.*)

MICHAEL (*going after him*). Is it yourself is fearing the polis? You're wanting,[32] maybe?

CHRISTY. There's many wanting.

MICHAEL. Many surely, with the broken harvest and the ended wars.[33] (*He picks up some stockings, etc.,*

[30] **polis** police [31] **bona fide** a genuine traveler, i.e., one who having traveled four or more miles could be served after licensing hours [32] **wanting** wanted by police [33] **ended wars** perhaps both the Land Wars (1879-82) and the Boer War (1899-1902)

that are near the fire, and carries them away furtively.)
It should be larceny, I'm thinking?

CHRISTY (*dolefully*). I had it in my mind it was a different word and a bigger.

PEGEEN. There's a queer lad. Were you never slapped in school, young fellow, that you don't know the name of your deed?

CHRISTY (*bashfully*). I'm slow at learning, a middling scholar only.

MICHAEL. If you're a dunce itself, you'd have a right to know that larceny's robbing and stealing. Is it for the like of that you're wanting?

CHRISTY (*with a flash of family pride*). And I the son of a strong farmer[34] (*with a sudden qualm*), God rest his soul, could have bought up the whole of your old house a while since, from the butt of his tail-pocket,[35] and not have missed the weight of it gone.

MICHAEL (*impressed*). If it's not stealing, it's maybe something big.

CHRISTY (*flattered*). Aye; it's maybe something big.

JIMMY. He's a wicked-looking young fellow. Maybe he followed after a young woman on a lonesome night.

CHRISTY (*shocked*). Oh, the saints forbid, mister; I was all times a decent lad.

PHILLY (*turning on* JIMMY). You're a silly man, Jimmy Farrell. He said his father was a farmer a while since, and there's himself now in a poor state. Maybe the land was grabbed [36] from him, and he did what any decent man would do.

MICHAEL (*to* CHRISTY, *mysteriously*). Was it bailiffs? [37]

CHRISTY. The divil a one.[38]

---

[34] strong farmer a well-to-do farmer with a large farm and much cattle   [35] tail-pocket of the old-fashioned swallow-tailed coat   [36] land was grabbed the common landlord practice of seizing tenant's land and evicting him for failing to pay the "rack-rent;" an action often attended with the most inhuman cruelty, rapine, and murder   [37] bailiffs district officials charged with collecting the tax   [38] divil a one strong negative

MICHAEL. Agents? [39]

CHRISTY. The divil a one.

MICHAEL. Landlords?

CHRISTY (*peevishly*). Ah, not at all, I'm saying. You'd see the like of them stories on any little paper of a Munster[40] town. But I'm not calling to mind any person, gentle, simple, judge or jury, did the like of me.

(*They all draw nearer with delighted curiosity.*)

PHILLY. Well, that lad's a puzzle-the-world.

JIMMY. He'd beat Dan Davies' circus, or the holy missioners making sermons on the villainy of man. Try him again, Philly.

PHILLY. Did you strike golden guineas[41] out of solder, young fellow, or shilling coins itself?

CHRISTY. I did not mister, not sixpence nor a farthing[42] coin.

JIMMY. Did you marry three wives maybe? I'm told there's a sprinkling have done that among the holy Luthers[43] of the preaching north.

CHRISTY (*shyly*). I never married with one, let alone with a couple or three.

PHILLY. Maybe he went fighting for the Boers,[44] the like of the man beyond, was judged to be hanged, quartered and drawn. Were you off east, young fellow, fighting bloody wars for Kruger[45] and the freedom of the Boers?

CHRISTY. I never left my own parish till Tuesday was a week.[46]

[39] **Agents** landlord representatives serving process on tenants failing to pay "the rent." The reference is to what Chesterfield called "the deputy of deputy of deputy system of land tenure." [40] **Munster** South-Western province of Ireland including Kerry [41] **golden guineas** old English coin once worth 21 shillings [42] **farthing** coin worth one-quarter of English penny [43] **holy Luthers** Presbyterians [44] **Boers** South African War (1899-1902); the Boers had a number of Irish Brigades fighting the British [45] **Kruger** Stephen, J. P. (1825-1904), South African statesman and leader of 1880 Boer Rebellion [46] **till Tuesday was a week** a week ago Tuesday

PEGEEN (*coming from counter*). He's done nothing, so. (*To* CHRISTY) If you didn't commit murder or a bad, nasty thing, or false coining, or robbery, or butchery, or the like of them, there isn't anything that would be worth your troubling for to run from now. You did nothing at all.

CHRISTY (*his feelings hurt*). That's an unkindly thing to be saying to a poor orphaned traveller, has a prison behind him, and hanging before, and hell's gap gaping below.

PEGEEN (*with a sign to the men to be quiet*). You're only saying it. You did nothing at all. A soft lad the like of you wouldn't slit the windpipe of a screeching sow.

CHRISTY (*offended*). You're not speaking the truth.

PEGEEN (*in mock rage*). Not speaking the truth, is it? Would you have me knock the head of you with the butt of the broom?

CHRISTY (*twisting round on her with a sharp cry of horror*). Don't strike me. I killed my poor father, Tuesday was a week, for doing the like of that.

PEGEEN (*with blank amazement*). Is it killed your father?

CHRISTY (*subsiding*). With the help of God I did surely, and that the Holy Immaculate Mother may intercede for his soul.

PHILLY (*retreating with* JIMMY). There's a daring fellow.

JIMMY. Oh, glory be to God!

MICHAEL (*with great respect*). That was a hanging crime, mister honey. You should have had good reason for doing the like of that.

CHRISTY (*in a very reasonable tone*). He was a dirty man, God forgive him, and he getting old and crusty, the way I couldn't put up with him at all.

PEGEEN. And you shot him dead?

CHRISTY (*shaking his head*). I never used weapons. I've no licence, and I'm a law-fearing man.

MICHAEL. It was with a hilted knife maybe? I'm told,

in the big world, it's bloody knives they use.

CHRISTY (*loudly, scandalized*). Do you take me for a slaughter-boy?

PEGEEN. You never hanged him, the way Jimmy Farrell hanged his dog from the licence,[47] and had it screeching and wriggling three hours at the butt of a string, and himself swearing it was a dead dog, and the peelers swearing it had life?

CHRISTY. I did not then. I just riz[48] the loy[49] and let fall the edge of it on the ridge of his skull, and he went down at my feet like an empty sack, and never let a grunt or groan from him at all.

MICHAEL (*making a sign to* PEGEEN *to fill* CHRISTY's *glass*). And what way weren't you hanged, mister? Did you bury him then?

CHRISTY (*considering*). Aye. I buried him then. Wasn't I digging spuds in the field?

MICHAEL. And the peelers never followed after you the eleven days that you're out?

CHRISTY (*shaking his head*). Never a one of them, and I walking forward facing hog, dog, or divil on the highway of the road.

PHILLY (*nodding wisely*). It's only with a common week-day kind of a murderer them lads would be trusting their carcase, and that man should be a great terror when his temper's roused.

MICHAEL. He should then. (*To* CHRISTY) And where was it, mister honey, that you did the deed?

CHRISTY (*looking at him with suspicion*). Oh, a distant place, master of the house, a windy corner of high distant hills.

PHILLY (*nodding with approval*). He's a close man,[50] and he's right surely.

PEGEEN. That'd be a lad with the sense of Solomon

---

[47] **from the licence** on account of the dog licence fee which he either would not or could not pay [48] **riz** raised; an example of strong inflection preferred by the Irish [49] **loy** a long narrow spade [50] **close man** a tight-lipped man

to have for a pot-boy, Michael James, if it's the truth you're seeking one at all.

PHILLY. The peelers is fearing him, and if you'd that lad in the house there isn't one of them would come smelling around if the dogs itself were lapping poteen[51] from the dung-pit of the yard.

JIMMY. Bravery's a treasure in a lonesome place, and a lad would kill his father, I'm thinking, would face a foxy divil with a pitchpike[52] on the flags of hell.

PEGEEN. It's the truth they're saying, and if I'd that lad in the house, I wouldn't be fearing the loosèd kharki cut-throats,[53] or the walking dead.

CHRISTY (*swelling with surprise and triumph*). Well, glory be to God!

MICHAEL (*with deference*). Would you think well to stop here and be pot-boy, mister honey, if we gave you good wages, and didn't destroy you with the weight of work?

SHAWN (*coming forward uneasily*). That'd be a queer kind to bring into a decent quiet household with the like of Pegeen Mike.

PEGEEN (*very sharply*). Will you wisht? Who's speaking to you?

SHAWN (*retreating*). A bloody-handed murderer the like of . . .

PEGEEN (*snapping at him*). Whisht I am saying; we'll take no fooling from your like at all. (*To* CHRISTY *with a honeyed voice*) And you, young fellow, you'd have a right to stop, I'm thinking, for we'd do our all and utmost to content your needs.

CHRISTY (*overcome with wonder*). And I'd be safe this place from the searching law?

MICHAEL. You would, surely. If they're not fearing you, itself, the peelers in this place is decent droughty[54] poor fellows, wouldn't touch a cur dog and not give warning in the dead of night.

[51] **poteen** illicit whiskey   [52] **pitchpike** pitchfork   [53] **loosèd kharki cut-throats** the English Garrison   [54] **droughty** thirsty

PEGEEN (*very kindly and persuasively*). Let you stop a short while anyhow. Aren't you destroyed walking with your feet in bleeding blisters, and your whole skin needing washing like a Wicklow sheep.

CHRISTY (*looking round with satisfaction*). It's a nice room, and if it's not humbugging me you are, I'm thinking that I'll surely stay.

JIMMY (*jumps up*). Now, by the grace of God, herself [55] will be safe this night, with a man killed his father holding danger from the door, and let you come on, Michael James, or they'll have the best stuff drunk at the wake.

MICHAEL (*going to the door with men*). And begging your pardon, mister, what name will we call you, for we'd like to know?

CHRISTY. Christopher Mahon.

MICHAEL. Well, God bless you, Christy, and a good rest till we meet again when the sun'll be rising to the noon of day.

CHRISTY. God bless you all.

MEN. God bless you.

(*They go out except* SHAWN, *who lingers at door.*)

SHAWN (*to* PEGEEN). Are you wanting me to stop along with you and keep you from harm?

PEGEEN (*gruffly*). Didn't you say you were fearing Father Reilly?

SHAWN. There'd be no harm staying now, I'm thinking, and himself in it [56] too.

PEGEEN. You wouldn't stay when there was need for you, and let you step off nimble this time when there's none.

SHAWN. Didn't I say it was Father Reilly . . .

PEGEEN. Go on, then, to Father Reilly (*in a jeering tone*), and let him put you in the holy brotherhoods,[57] and leave that lad to me.

---

[55] **herself** Pegeen [56] **himself in it** Christy here [57] **holy brotherhoods** religious groups of men with vows of poverty, chastity, and obedience

SHAWN. If I meet the Widow Quin . . .

PEGEEN. Go on, I'm saying, and don't be waking this place with your noise. (*She hustles him out and bolts door.*) That lad would wear the spirits from the saints of peace. (*Bustles about, then takes off her apron and pins it up in the window as a blind.* CHRISTY *watching her timidly. Then she comes to him and speaks with bland good-humour.*) Let you stretch out now by the fire, young fellow. You should be destroyed travelling.

CHRISTY (*shyly again, drawing off his boots*). I'm tired surely, walking wild eleven days, and waking fearful in the night.

(*He holds up one of his feet, feeling his blisters, and looking at them with compassion.*)

PEGEEN (*standing beside him, watching him with delight*). You should have had great people in your family, I'm thinking, with the little, small feet you have, and you with a kind of a quality name,[58] the like of what you'd find on the great powers and potentates of France and Spain.

CHRISTY (*with pride*). We were great surely, with wide and windy acres of rich Munster land.

PEGEEN. Wasn't I telling you, and you a fine, handsome young fellow with a noble brow?

CHRISTY (*with a flash of delighted surprise*). Is it me?

PEGEEN. Aye. Did you never hear that from the young girls where you come from in the west or south?

CHRISTY (*with venom*). I did not then. Oh, they're bloody[59] liars in the naked parish where I grew a man.

PEGEEN. If they are itself, you've heard it these days, I'm thinking, and you walking the world telling out your story to young girls or old.

CHRISTY. I've told my story no place till this night,

[58] **quality name** a gentry name, an aristocrat   [59] **bloody** in the West a mild expletive like beastly or bloomin'. Recall the furor over Shaw's use of it in *Pygmalion*

Pegeen Mike, and it's foolish I was here, maybe, to be talking free, but you're decent people, I'm thinking, and yourself a kindly woman, the way I wasn't fearing you at all.

PEGEEN (*filling a sack with straw*). You've said the like of that, maybe, in every cot[60] and cabin where you've met a young girl on your way.

CHRISTY (*going over to her, gradually raising his voice*). I've said it nowhere till this night, I'm telling you, for I've seen none the like of you the eleven long days I am walking the world, looking over a low ditch or a high ditch on my north or south, into stony scattered fields, or scribes[61] of bog, where you'd see young, limber girls, and fine prancing women making laughter with the men.

PEGEEN. If you weren't destroyed travelling, you'd have as much talk and streeleen,[62] I'm thinking, as Owen Roe O'Sullivan[63] or the poets of the Dingle Bay,[64] and I've heard all times it's the poets are your like, fine fiery fellows with great rages when their temper's roused.

CHRISTY (*drawing a little nearer to her*). You've a power[65] of rings, God bless you, and would there be any offence if I was asking are you single now?

PEGEEN. What would I want wedding so young?

CHRISTY (*with relief*). We're alike, so.

PEGEEN (*she puts sack on settle and beats it up*). I never killed my father. I'd be afeard to do that, except I was the like of yourself with blind rages tearing me within, for I'm thinking you should have had great tussling when the end was come.

CHRISTY (*expanding with delight at the first confidential talk he has ever had with a woman*). We had not then. It was a hard woman[66] was come over the

---

[60] **cot** a small cabin or cottage [61] **scribes** long and narrow strips of arable land [62] **streeleen** chatter [63] **Owen Roe O'Sullivan** 18th century Kerry poet, something of a playboy himself [64] **Dingle Bay** a large inlet of the Kerry coast [65] **a power a** large quantity [66] **hard woman** dreadful woman

hill, and if he was always a crusty kind when he'd a hard woman setting him on, not the divil himself or his four fathers[67] could put up with him at all.

PEGEEN (*with curiosity*). And isn't it a great wonder that one wasn't fearing you?

CHRISTY (*very confidentially*). Up to the day I killed my father, there wasn't a person in Ireland knew the kind I was, and I there drinking, waking, eating, sleeping, a quiet, simple poor fellow with no man giving me heed.

PEGEEN (*getting a quilt out of cupboard and putting it on the sack*). It was the girls were giving you heed maybe, and I'm thinking it's most conceit you'd have to be gaming[68] with their like.

CHRISTY (*shaking his head, with simplicity*). Not the girls itself, and I won't tell you a lie. There wasn't anyone heeding me in that place saving only the dumb beasts of the field.   (*He sits down at fire.*)

PEGEEN (*with disappointment*). And I thinking you should have been living the like of a king of Norway or the eastern world.[69]

(*She comes and sits beside him after placing bread and mug of milk on the table.*)

CHRISTY (*laughing piteously*). The like of a king, is it? And I after toiling, moiling,[70] digging, dodging[71] from the dawn till dusk with never a sight of joy or sport saving only when I'd be abroad in the dark night poaching rabbits on hills, for I was a divil to poach, God forgive me, (*very naively*) and I near got six months for going with a dung fork and stabbing a fish.

PEGEEN. And it's that you'd call sport, is it, to be abroad in the darkness with yourself alone?

CHRISTY. I did, God help me, and there I'd be as happy as the sunshine of St. Martin's Day,[72] watching

[67] **four fathers** whole family   [68] **gaming** fooling   [69] **eastern world** a sort of wonderland in Irish folktales   [70] **moiling** working hard   [71] **dodging** going at a slow pace over a small job   [72] **St. Martin's Day** November 11th

the light passing the north or the patches of fog, till
I'd hear a rabbit starting to screech and I'd go running in the furze. Then when I'd my full share I'd
come walking down where you'd see the ducks and
geese stretched sleeping on the highway of the road,
and before I'd pass the dunghill, I'd hear himself snor-
ing out, a loud lonesome snore he'd be making all
times, the while he was sleeping, and he a man'd be
raging all times, the while he was waking, like a gaudy
officer you'd hear cursing and damning and swearing
oaths.

PEGEEN. Providence and Mercy, spare us all!

CHRISTY. It's that you'd say surely if you seen him
and he after drinking for weeks, rising up in the red
dawn, or before it maybe, and going out into the yard
as naked as an ash tree in the moon of May, and shying
clods against the visage of the stars till he'd put the
fear of death into the banbhs[73] and the screeching
sows.

PEGEEN. I'd be well-nigh afeard of that lad myself,
I'm thinking. And there was no one in it but the two
of you alone?

CHRISTY. The divil a one, though he'd sons and
daughters walking all great states and territories of the
world, and not a one of them, to this day, but would
say their seven curses on him, and they rousing up to
let a cough or sneeze, maybe, in the deadness of the
night.

PEGEEN (*nodding her head*). Well, you should have
been a queer lot. I never cursed my father the like of
that, though I'm twenty and more years of age.

CHRISTY. Then you'd have cursed mine, I'm telling
you, and he a man never gave peace to any, saving
when he'd get two months or three, or be locked in
the asylums for battering peelers or assaulting men,
(*with depression*) the way it was a bitter life he led
me till I did up a Tuesday and halve his skull.

PEGEEN (*putting her hand on his shoulder*). Well,
[73] banbhs young pigs

you'll have peace in this place, Christy Mahon, and none to trouble you, and it's near time a fine lad like you should have your good share of the earth.

CHRISTY. It's time surely, and I a seemly fellow with great strength in me and bravery of . . .

(Some one knocks)

CHRISTY *(clinging to* PEGEEN*)*. Oh, glory! it's late for knocking, and this last while I'm in terror of the peelers, and the walking dead.

(Knocking again.)

PEGEEN. Who's there?

VOICE *(outside)*. Me.

PEGEEN. Who's me?

VOICE. The Widow Quin.

PEGEEN *(jumping up and giving him the bread and milk)*. Go on now with your supper, and let on[74] to be sleepy, for if she found you were such a warrant to talk, she'd be stringing gabble till the dawn of day.

(He takes bread and sits shyly with his back to the door.)

PEGEEN *(opening door, with temper)*. What ails you, or what is it you're wanting at this hour of the night?

WIDOW QUIN *(coming in a step and peering at* CHRISTY*)*. I'm after meeting Shawn Keogh and Father Reilly below, who told me of your curiosity man, and they fearing by this time he was maybe roaring, romping on your hands with drink.

PEGEEN *(pointing to* CHRISTY*)*. Look now is he roaring, and he stretched out drowsy with his supper and his mug of milk. Walk down and tell that to Father Reilly and to Shaneen Keogh.

WIDOW QUIN *(coming forward)*. I'll not see them again, for I've their word[75] to lead that lad forward for to lodge with me.

PEGEEN *(in blank amazement)*. This night, is it?

[74] **let on** pretend   [75] **word** their orders

WIDOW QUIN (*going over*). This night. "It isn't fitting," says the priesteen,[76] "to have his likeness lodging with an orphaned girl." (*To* CHRISTY) God save you, mister!

CHRISTY (*shyly*). God save you kindly.

WIDOW QUIN (*looking at him with half-amused curiosity*). Well, aren't you a little smiling fellow? It should have been great and bitter torments did rouse your spirits to a deed of blood.

CHRISTY (*doubtfully*). It should, maybe.

WIDOW QUIN. It's more than "maybe" I'm saying, and it'd soften my heart to see you sitting so simple with your cup and cake, and you fitter to be saying your catechism than slaying your da.[77]

PEGEEN (*at counter, washing glasses*). There's talking[78] when any'd see he's fit to be holding his head high with the wonders of the world. Walk on from this, for I'll not have him tormented and he destroyed travelling since Tuesday was a week.

WIDOW QUIN (*peaceably*). We'll be walking surely when his supper's done, and you'll find we're great company, young fellow, when it's of the like of you and me you'd hear the penny poets[79] singing in an August Fair.

CHRISTY (*innocently*). Did you kill your father?

PEGEEN (*contemptuously*). She did not. She hit himself [80] with a worn pick, and the rusted poison did corrode his blood the way he never overed it,[81] and died after. That was a sneaky kind of murder did win small glory with the boys itself.

(*She crosses to* CHRISTY's *left.*)

WIDOW QUIN (*with good-humour*). If it didn't, maybe all knows a widow woman has buried her chil-

---

[76] **priesteen** little priest, used contemptuously [77] **da** father [78] **There's talking** ironically—grand talk, great talk [79] **penny poets** ballad-singers [80] **himself** her husband [81] **overed it** recovered

dren and destroyed her man is a wiser comrade for a young lad than a girl, the like of you, who'd go helter-skeltering after any man would let you a wink upon the road.

PEGEEN (*breaking out into wild rage*). And you'll say that, Widow Quin, and you gasping with the rage you had racing the hill beyond to look on his face.

WIDOW QUIN (*laughing derisively*). Me, is it? Well, Father Reilly has cuteness[82] to divide you now. (*She pulls* CHRISTY *up.*) There's great temptation in a man did slay his da, and we'd best be going, young fellow; so rise up and come with me.

PEGEEN (*seizing his arm*). He'll not stir. He's pot-boy in this place, and I'll not have him stolen off and kidnapped while himself's abroad.

WIDOW QUIN. It'd be a crazy pot-boy'd lodge him in the shebeen[83] where he works by day, so you'd have a right to come on, young fellow, till you see my little houseen,[84] a perch off on the rising hill.

PEGEEN. Wait till morning, Christy Mahon. Wait till you lay eyes on her leaky thatch is growing more pasture[85] for her buck goat than her square of fields, and she without a tramp itself to keep in order her place at all.

WIDOW QUIN. When you see me contriving in my little gardens, Christy Mahon, you'll swear the Lord God formed me to be living lone, and that there isn't my match in Mayo for thatching, or mowing, or shearing a sheep.

PEGEEN (*with noisy scorn*). It's true the Lord God formed you to contrive indeed. Doesn't the world know you reared a black ram at your own breast, so that the Lord Bishop of Connaught felt the elements of a Christian, and he eating it after in a kidney stew? Doesn't

---

[82] **cuteness** sharpness or ingenuity [83] **shebeen** an unlicensed place where intoxicating liquors are sold [84] **houseen** little house [85] **pasture** her thatch roof has been up so long that grass has taken root there

the world know you've been shaving the foxy skipper from France[86] for a threepenny bit and a sop of grass tobacco would wring the liver from a mountain goat you'd meet leaping the hills?

WIDOW QUIN (*with amusement*). Do you hear her now, young fellow? Do you hear the way she'll be rating at your own self when a week is by?

PEGEEN (*to* CHRISTY). Don't heed her. Tell her to go on into her pigsty and not plague us here.

WIDOW QUIN. I'm going; but he'll come with me.

PEGEEN (*shaking him*). Are you dumb, young fellow?

CHRISTY (*timidly, to* WIDOW QUIN). God increase you;[87] but I'm pot-boy in this place, and it's here I'd liefer[88] stay.

PEGEEN (*triumphantly*). Now you have heard him, and go on from this.

WIDOW QUIN (*looking round the room*). It's lonesome this hour crossing the hill, and if he won't come along with me, I'd have a right maybe to stop this night with yourselves. Let me stretch out on the settle, Pegeen Mike; and himself can lie by the hearth.

PEGEEN (*short and fiercely*). Faith,[89] I won't. Quit off [90] or I will send you now.

WIDOW QUIN (*gathering her shawl up*). Well, it's a terror to be aged a score. (*To* CHRISTY) God bless you now, young fellow, and let you be wary, or there's right torment will await you here if you go romancing with her like, and she waiting only, as they bade me say, on a sheepskin parchment[91] to be wed with Shawn Keogh of Killakeen.

CHRISTY (*going to* PEGEEN *as she bolts door*). What's that she's after saying?

PEGEEN. Lies and blather, you've no call to mind. Well, isn't Shawn Keogh an impudent fellow to send

---

[86] **skipper from France** from French trawlers fishing off the coast
[87] **God increase you** meaning your substance, an Irish blessing
[88] **liefer** rather [89] **Faith** in faith, not to be used lightly [90] **Quit off** get out [91] **sheepskin parchment** the dispensation

up spying on me? Wait till I lay hands on him. Let him wait, I'm saying.

CHRISTY. And you're not wedding him at all?

PEGEEN. I wouldn't wed him if a bishop came walking for to join us here.

CHRISTY. That God in glory may be thanked for that.

PEGEEN. There's your bed now. I've put a quilt upon you I'm after quilting a while since[92] with my own two hands, and you'd best stretch out now for your sleep, and may God give you a good rest till I call you in the morning when the cocks will crow.

CHRISTY (*as she goes to inner room*). May God and Mary and St. Patrick bless you and reward you, for your kindly talk. (*She shuts the door behind her. He settles his bed slowly, feeling the quilt with immense satisfaction.*) Well, it's a clean bed and soft with it,[93] and it's great luck and company I've won me in the end of time—two fine women fighting for the likes of me—till I'm thinking this night wasn't I a foolish fellow not to kill my father in the years gone by.

CURTAIN

Act II

SCENE: *As before. Brilliant morning light.* CHRISTY, *looking bright and cheerful, is cleaning a girl's boots.*

CHRISTY (*to himself, counting jugs on dresser*). Half a hundred beyond. Ten there. A score that's above. Eighty jugs. Six cups and a broken one. Two plates. A power of glasses. Bottles, a schoolmaster'd be hard set to count, and enough in them, I'm thinking, to drunken all the wealth and wisdom of the County Clare.[1] (*He puts down the boot carefully.*) There's her

---

[92] **a while since** a while ago   [93] **soft with it** soft too
[1] **County Clare** Western county bordering the Atlantic between Galway and Kerry

boots now, nice and decent for her evening use, and isn't it grand brushes she has? (*He puts them down and goes by degrees to the looking-glass.*) Well, this'd be a fine place to be my whole life talking out with swearing Christians, in place of my old dogs and cat, and I stalking around, smoking my pipe and drinking my fill, and never a day's work but drawing a cork an odd time, or wiping a glass, or rinsing out a shiny tumbler for a decent man. (*He takes the looking-glass from the wall and puts it on the back of a chair; then sits down in front of it and begins washing his face.*) Didn't I know rightly I was handsome, though it was the divil's own mirror we had beyond, would twist a squint across an angel's brow, and I'll be growing fine from this day, the way I'll have a soft lovely skin on me and won't be the like of the clumsy young fellows do be ploughing all times in the earth and dung. (*He starts.*) Is she coming again? (*He looks out.*) Stranger girls. God help me, where'll I hide myself away and my long neck naked to the world? (*He looks out.*) I'd best go to the room maybe till I'm dressed again.

(*He gathers up his coat and the looking-glass, and runs into the inner room. The door is pushed open, and* SUSAN BRADY *looks in, and knocks on door.*)

SUSAN. There's nobody in it. (*Knocks again*)

NELLY (*pushing her in and following her, with* HONOR BLAKE *and* SARA TANSEY). It'd be early for them both to be out walking the hill.

SUSAN. I'm thinking Shawn Keogh was making game of us and there's no such man in it at all.

HONOR (*pointing to straw and quilt*). Look at that. He's been sleeping there in the night. Well, it'll be a hard case[2] if he's gone off now, the way we'll never set our eyes on a man killed his father, and we after rising early and destroying ourselves running fast on the hill.

[2] **a hard case** a sad state of affairs

NELLY. Are you thinking them's his boots?

SARA (*taking them up*). If they are, there should be his father's track on them. Did you never read in the papers the way murdered men do bleed and drip?

SUSAN. Is that blood there, Sara Tansey?

SARA (*smelling it*). That's bog water, I'm thinking, but it's his own they are surely, for I never seen the like of them for whitey mud, and red mud, and turf on them, and the fine sands of the sea. That man's been walking, I'm telling you.

(*She goes down right, putting on one of his boots.*)

SUSAN (*going to window*). Maybe he's stolen off to Belmullet[3] with the boots of Michael James, and you'd have a right so to follow after him, Sara Tansey, and you the one yoked the ass cart and drove ten miles to set your eyes on the man bit the yellow lady's nostril on the northern shore.   (*She looks out.*)

SARA (*running to window, with one boot on*). Don't be talking, and we fooled to-day. (*Putting on the other boot*) There's a pair do fit me well, and I'll be keeping them for walking to the priest, when you'd be ashamed this place, going up winter and summer with nothing worth while to confess at all.

HONOR (*who has been listening at door*). Whisht! there's some one inside the room. (*She pushes door a chink open.*) It's a man.

(*Sara kicks off boots and puts them where they were. They all stand in a line looking through chink.*)

SARA. I'll call him. Mister! Mister! (*He puts in his head.*) Is Pegeen within?

CHRISTY (*coming in as meek as a mouse, with the looking-glass held behind his back*). She's above on the cnuceen,[4] seeking the nanny goats, the way she'd have a sup of goat's milk for to colour my tea.

[3] **Belmullet** small seaport on Mullet peninsula   [4] **cnuceen** Irish for little hill

SARA. And asking your pardon, is it you's the man killed his father?

CHRISTY (*sidling toward the nail where the glass was hanging*). I am, God help me!

SARA (*taking eggs she has brought*). Then my thousand welcomes to you, and I've run up with a brace of duck's eggs for your food to-day. Pegeen's ducks is no use, but these are the real rich sort. Hold out your hand and you'll see it's no lie I'm telling you.

CHRISTY (*coming forward shyly, and holding out his left hand*). They're a great and weighty size.

SUSAN. And I run up with a pat of butter, for it'd be a poor thing to have you eating your spuds dry, and you after running a great way since you did destroy your da.

CHRISTY. Thank you kindly.

HONOR. And I brought you a little cut of a cake, for you should have a thin stomach on you, and you that length walking the world.

NELLY. And I brought you a little laying pullet—boiled and all she is—was crushed at the fall of night by the curate's car. Feel the fat of that breast, Mister.

CHRISTY. It's bursting, surely.

(*He feels it with the back of his hand, in which he holds the presents.*)

SARA. Will you pinch it? Is your right hand too sacred for to use at all? (*She slips round behind him.*) It's a glass he has. Well, I never seen to this day a man with a looking-glass held to his back. Them that kills their fathers is a vain lot surely. (GIRLS *giggle.*)

CHRISTY (*smiling innocently and piling presents on glass*). I'm very thankful to you all to-day. . . .

WIDOW QUIN (*coming in quickly, at door.*) Sara Tansey, Susan Brady, Honor Blake! What in glory has you here at this hour of day?

GIRLS (*giggling*). That's the man killed his father.

WIDOW QUIN (*coming to them*). I know well it's the

man; and I'm after putting him down in the sports below for racing, leaping, pitching, and the Lord knows what.

SARA (*exuberantly*). That's right, Widow Quin. I'll bet my dowry that he'll lick the world.

WIDOW QUIN. If you will, you'd have a right to have him fresh and nourished in place of nursing a feast. (*Taking presents*) Are you fasting or fed, young fellow?

CHRISTY. Fasting, if you please.

WIDOW QUIN (*loudly*). Well, you're the lot. Stir up now and give him his breakfast. (*To* CHRISTY) Come here to me (*she puts him on bench beside her while the girls make tea and get his breakfast*) and let you tell us your story before Pegeen will come, in place of grinning your ears off like the moon of May.

CHRISTY (*beginning to be pleased*). It's a long story; you'd be destroyed listening.

WIDOW QUIN. Don't be letting on to be shy, a fine, gamey,[5] treacherous lad the like of you. Was it in your house beyond you cracked his skull?

CHRISTY (*shy but flattered*). It was not. We were digging spuds in his cold, sloping, stony, divil's patch of a field.

WIDOW QUIN. And you went asking money of him, or making talk of getting a wife would drive him from his farm?

CHRISTY. I did not, then; but there I was, digging and digging, and "You squinting idiot," says he, "let you walk down now and tell the priest you'll wed the Widow Casey in a score of days."

WIDOW QUIN. And what kind was she?

CHRISTY (*with horror*). A walking terror from beyond the hills, and she two score and five years, and two hundredweights and five pounds in the weighing scales, with a limping leg on her, and a blinded eye, and she a woman of noted misbehaviour with the old and young.

[5] **gamey** merry

GIRLS (*clustering round him, serving him*). Glory be.

WIDOW QUIN. And what did he want driving you to wed her?

(*She takes a bit of the chicken.*)

CHRISTY (*eating with growing satisfaction*). He was letting on I was wanting a protector from the harshness of the world, and he without a thought the whole while but how he'd have her hut to live in and her gold to drink.

WIDOW QUIN. There's maybe worse than a dry hearth and a widow woman and your glass at night. So you hit him then?

CHRISTY (*getting almost excited*). I did not. "I won't wed her," says I, "when all know she did suckle me for six weeks when I came into the world, and she a hag this day with a tongue on her has the crows and seabirds scattered, the way they wouldn't cast a shadow on her garden with the dread of her curse."

WIDOW QUIN (*teasingly*). That one should be right company.

SARA (*eagerly*). Don't mind her. Did you kill him then?

CHRISTY. "She's too good for the like of you," says he, "and go on now or I'll flatten you out like a crawling beast has passed under a dray." [6] "You will not if I can help it," says I. "Go on," says he, "or I'll have the divil making garters of your limbs to-night." "You will not if I can help it," says I. (*He sits up, brandishing his mug.*)

SARA. You were right surely.

CHRISTY (*impressively*). With that the sun came out between the cloud and the hill, and it shining green in my face. "God have mercy on your soul," says he, lifting a scythe; "or on your own," says I, raising the loy.

SUSAN. That's a grand story.

⁰ **dray** a little cart with or without wheels

HONOR. He tells it lovely.

CHRISTY (*flattered and confident, waving bone*). He gave a drive with the scythe, and I gave a lep[7] to the east. Then I turned around with my back to the north, and I hit a blow on the ridge of his skull, laid him stretched out, and he split to the knob of his gullet.

(*He raises the chicken bone to his Adam's apple.*)

GIRLS (*together*). Well, you're a marvel! Oh, God bless you! You're the lad surely!

SUSAN. I'm thinking the Lord God sent him this road to make a second husband to the Widow Quin, and she with a great yearning to be wedded, though all dread her here. Lift him on her knee, Sara Tansey.

WIDOW QUIN. Don't tease him.

SARA (*going over to dresser and counter very quickly, and getting two glasses and porter*). You're heroes surely, and let you drink a supeen[8] with your arms linked like the outlandish lovers in the sailor's song. (*She links their arms and gives them the glasses.*) There now. Drink a health to the wonders of the western world,[9] the pirates, preachers, poteen-makers, with the jobbing jockies;[10] parching peelers, and the juries fill their stomachs selling judgments of the English law.

(*Brandishing the bottle*)

WIDOW QUIN. That's a right toast, Sara Tansey. Now Christy.

(*They drink with their arms linked, he drinking with his left hand, she with her right. As they are drinking, PEGEEN MIKE comes in with a milk can and stands aghast. They all spring away from CHRISTY. He goes down left. WIDOW QUIN remains seated.*)

PEGEEN (*angrily to SARA*). What is it you're wanting?

SARA (*twisting her apron*). An ounce of tobacco.

[7] **lep** a leap [8] **supeen** a little sup [9] **western world** western Ireland [10] **jobbing jockies** men who go round breaking in horses

PEGEEN. Have you tuppence?[11]

SARA. I've forgotten my purse.

PEGEEN. Then you'd best be getting it and not be fooling us here. (*To the* WIDOW QUIN, *with more elaborate scorn*) And what is it you're wanting, Widow Quin?

WIDOW QUIN (*insolently*). A penn'orth[12] of starch.

PEGEEN (*breaking out*). And you without a white shift[13] or a shirt in your whole family since the drying of the flood. I've no starch for the like of you, and let you walk on now to Killamuck.

WIDOW QUIN (*turning to* CHRISTY, *as she goes out with the girls*). Well, you're mighty huffy this day, Pegeen Mike, and, you young fellow, let you not forget the sports and racing when the noon is by.

(*They go out.*)

PEGEEN (*imperiously*). Fling out that rubbish and put them cups away. (CHRISTY *tidies away in great haste.*) Shove in the bench by the wall. (*He does so.*) And hang that glass[14] on the nail. What disturbed it at all?

CHRISTY (*very meekly*). I was making myself decent only, and this a fine country for young lovely girls.

PEGEEN (*sharply*). Whisht your talking of girls.

(*Goes to counter on right*)

CHRISTY. Wouldn't any wish to be decent in a place . . .

PEGEEN. Whisht I'm saying.

CHRISTY (*looks at her face for a moment with great misgivings, then as a last effort, takes up a loy, and goes towards her, with feigned assurance*). It was with a loy the like of that I killed my father.

PEGEEN (*still sharply*). You've told me that story six times since the dawn of day.

CHRISTY (*reproachfully*). It's a queer thing you

[11] **tuppence** two pence   [12] **penn'orth** penny worth   [13] **shift** a woman's slip   [14] **glass** the mirror

wouldn't care to be hearing it and them girls after walking four miles to be listening to me now.

PEGEEN (*turning round astonished*). Four miles?

CHRISTY (*apologetically*). Didn't himself say there were only bona fides[15] living in the place?

PEGEEN. It's bona fides by the road they are, but that lot came over the river lepping[16] the stones. It's not three perches when you go like that, and I was down this morning looking on the papers the post-boy does have in his bag. (*With meaning and emphasis*) For there was great news this day, Christopher Mahon.

(*She goes into room on left.*)

CHRISTY (*suspiciously*). Is it news of my murder?

PEGEEN (*inside*). Murder, indeed.

CHRISTY (*loudly*). A murdered da?

PEGEEN (*coming in again and crossing right*). There was not, but a story filled half a page of the hanging of a man. Ah, that should be a fearful end, young fellow, and it worst of all for a man destroyed his da, for the like of him would get small mercies, and when it's dead he is, they'd put him in a narrow grave, with cheap sacking wrapping him round, and pour down quicklime on his head, the way you'd see a woman pouring any frish-frash[17] from a cup.

CHRISTY (*very miserably*). Oh, God help me. Are you thinking I'm safe? You were saying at the fall of night, I was shut of[18] jeopardy and I here with yourselves.

PEGEEN (*severely*). You'll be shut of jeopardy no place if you go talking with a pack of wild girls the

[15] **bona fides** earlier Michael James had reassured Christy that no one except a widow lived within four miles of his public house so that anyone coming at any hour could *bona fide* call for a drink and be served without prejudice to the licensing laws   [16] **lepping** leaping   [17] **frish-frash** a kind of Indian meal and raw cabbage boiled down as thin as gruel   [18] **shut of** to be rid of

like of them do be walking abroad with the peelers,
talking whispers at the fall of night.

CHRISTY (*with terror*). And you're thinking they'd
tell?

PEGEEN (*with mock sympathy*). Who knows, God
help you?

CHRISTY (*loudly*). What joy would they have to
bring hanging to the likes of me?

PEGEEN. It's queer joys they have, and who knows
the thing they'd do, if it'd make the green stones cry
itself to think of you swaying and swiggling at the
butt of a rope, and you with a fine, stout neck, God
bless you! the way you'd be a half an hour, in great
anguish, getting your death.

CHRISTY (*getting his boots and putting them on*).
If there's that terror of them, it'd be best, maybe, I
went on wandering like Esau[19] or Cain and Abel[20] on
the sides of Neifin[21] or the Erris plain.[22]

PEGEEN (*beginning to play with him*). It would,
maybe, for I've heard the Circuit Judges this place is
a heartless crew.

CHRISTY (*bitterly*). It's more than Judges this place
is a heartless crew. (*Looking up at her*) And isn't it a
poor thing to be starting again and I a lonesome fellow
will be looking out on women and girls the way the
needy fallen spirits do be looking on the Lord?

PEGEEN. What call[23] have you to be that lonesome
when there's poor girls walking Mayo in their thou-
sands now?

CHRISTY (*grimly*). It's well you know what call I
have. It's well you know it's a lonesome thing to be
passing small towns with the lights shining sideways

---

[19] **Esau** elder son of Isaac and Rebekah and brother of Jacob.
Christy, like Esau, has lost his birthright—the right to inherit
Old Mahon's "divil's patch," and so must provide for himself
[20] **Cain and Abel** Christy like Cain is guilty of murder and
now shares the curse of Cain to be a wanderer and a fugitive
on the face of the earth   [21] **Neifin** Mayo's Mount Nephin (Irish,
Néifin) just west of Lough Conn   [22] **Erris plain** the plain of
North Mayo   [23] **What call** what right

when the night is down, or going in strange places
with a dog noising before you and a dog noising behind, or drawn to the cities where you'd hear a voice
kissing and talking deep love in every shadow of the
ditch, and you passing on with an empty, hungry
stomach failing from your heart.

PEGEEN. I'm thinking you're an odd man, Christy
Mahon. The oddest walking fellow I ever set my eyes
on to this hour to-day.

CHRISTY. What would any be but odd men and they
living lonesome in the world?

PEGEEN. I'm not odd, and I'm my whole life with my
father only.

CHRISTY (*with infinite admiration*). How would a
lovely handsome woman the like of you be lonesome
when all men should be thronging around to hear the
sweetness of your voice, and the little infant children
should be pestering your steps I'm thinking, and you
walking the roads.

PEGEEN. I'm hard set to know what way a coaxing fellow the like of yourself should be lonesome
either.

CHRISTY. Coaxing?

PEGEEN. Would you have me think a man never
talked with the girls would have the words you've
spoken to-day? It's only letting on you are to be lonesome, the way you'd get around me now.

CHRISTY. I wish to God I was letting on; but I was
lonesome all times, and born lonesome, I'm thinking,
as the moon of dawn. (*Going to door*)

PEGEEN (*puzzled by his talk*). Well, it's a story I'm
not understanding at all why you'd be worse than another, Christy Mahon, and you a fine lad with the
great savagery to destroy your da.

CHRISTY. It's little I'm understanding myself, saving
only that my heart's scalded this day, and I going off
stretching out the earth between us, the way I'll not
be waking near you another dawn of the year till the
two of us do arise to hope or judgment with the saints

of God, and now I'd best be going with my wattle[24] in my hand, for hanging is a poor thing (*turning to go*), and it's little welcome only is left me in this house to-day.

PEGEEN (*sharply*). Christy! (*He turns round.*) Come here to me. (*He goes towards her.*) Lay down that switch and throw some sods on the fire. You're pot-boy in this place, and I'll not have you mitch off[25] from us now.

CHRISTY. You were saying I'd be hanged if I stay.

PEGEEN (*quite kindly at last*). I'm after going down and reading the fearful crimes of Ireland for two weeks or three, and there wasn't a word of your murder. (*Getting up and going over to the counter*) They've likely not found the body. You're safe so[26] with ourselves.

CHRISTY (*astonished, slowly*). It's making game of me you were (*following her with fearful joy*), and I can stay so, working at your side, and I not lonesome from this mortal day.

PEGEEN. What's to hinder you staying, except the widow woman or the young girls would inveigle[27] you off?

CHRISTY (*with rapture*). And I'll have your words from this day filling my ears, and that look is come upon you meeting my two eyes, and I watching you loafing around in the warm sun, or rinsing your ankles when the night is come.

PEGEEN (*kindly, but a little embarrassed*). I'm thinking you'll be a loyal young lad to have working around, and if you vexed me a while since with your leaguing[28] with the girls, I wouldn't give a thraneen[29] for a lad hadn't a mighty spirit in him and a gamey heart.

[24] **wattle** a short thick stick   [25] **mitch off** to sneak away, to play truant   [26] **safe so** in that case   [27] **inveigle** lure   [28] **leaguing** mixing with   [29] **thraneen** a straw, a withered stalk of meadow grass

(SHAWN KEOGH *runs in carrying a cleeve*[30] *on his back, followed by the* WIDOW QUIN.)

SHAWN (*to* PEGEEN). I was passing below, and I seen your mountainy sheep eating cabbages in Jimmy's field. Run up or they'll be bursting surely.

PEGEEN. Oh, God mend them![31]

(*She puts a shawl over her head and runs out.*)

CHRISTY (*looking from one to the other. Still in high spirits*). I'd best go to her aid maybe. I'm handy with ewes.

WIDOW QUIN (*closing the door*). She can do that much, and there is Shaneen has long speeches for to tell you now. (*She sits down with an amused smile.*)

SHAWN (*taking something from his pocket and offering it to* CHRISTY). Do you see that, mister?

CHRISTY (*looking at it*). The half of a ticket to the Western States![32]

SHAWN (*trembling with anxiety*). I'll give it to you and my new hat (*pulling it out of hamper*); and my breeches with the double seat (*pulling it out*); and my new coat is woven from the blackest shearings for three miles around (*giving him the coat*); I'll give you the whole of them, and my blessing, and the blessing of Father Reilly itself, maybe, if you'll quit from this and leave us in the peace we had till last night at the fall of dark.

CHRISTY (*with a new arrogance*). And for what is it you're wanting to get shut of me?

SHAWN (*looking to the* WIDOW *for help*). I'm a poor scholar with middling faculties to coin a lie, so I'll tell you the truth, Christy Mahon. I'm wedding with Pegeen beyond, and I don't think well of having a clever fearless man the like of you dwelling in her house.

---

[30] **cleeve** a basket, a creel   [31] **God mend them** serve them right
[32] **half . . . States** one-way ticket to America

CHRISTY (*almost pugnaciously*). And you'd be using bribery for to banish me?

SHAWN (*in an imploring voice*). Let you not take it badly, mister honey, isn't beyond the best place for you where you'll have golden chains and shiny coats and you riding upon hunters with the ladies of the land.

(*He makes an eager sign to the* WIDOW QUIN *to come to help him.*)

WIDOW QUIN (*coming over*). It's true for him, and you'd best quit off and not have that poor girl setting her mind on you, for there's Shaneen thinks she wouldn't suit you though all is saying that she'll wed you now.

(CHRISTY *beams with delight.*)

SHAWN (*in terrified earnest*). She wouldn't suit you, and she with the divil's own temper the way you'd be strangling one another in a score of days. (*He makes the movement of strangling with his hands.*) It's the like of me only that she's fit for, a quiet simple fellow wouldn't raise a hand upon her if she scratched itself.

WIDOW QUIN (*putting* SHAWN's *hat on* CHRISTY). Fit them clothes on you anyhow, young fellow, and he'd maybe loan them to you for the sports. (*Pushing him towards inner door*) Fit them on and you can give your answer when you have them tried.

CHRISTY (*beaming, delighted with the clothes*). I will then. I'd like herself to see me in them tweeds and hat.

(*He goes into room and shuts the door.*)

SHAWN (*in great anxiety*). He'd like herself to see them. He'll not leave us, Widow Quin. He's a score of divils in him the way it's well nigh certain he will wed Pegeen.

WIDOW QUIN (*jeeringly*). It's true all girls are fond of courage and do hate the like of you.

SHAWN (*walking about in desperation*). Oh, Widow

Quin, what'll I be doing now? I'd inform again him,[33] but he'd burst from Kilmainham[34] and he'd be sure and certain to destroy me. If I wasn't so God-fearing, I'd near have courage to come behind him and run a pike[35] into his side. Oh, it's a hard case to be an orphan and not to have your father that you're used to, and you'd easy kill and make yourself a hero in the sight of all. (*Coming up to her*) Oh, Widow Quin, will you find me some contrivance when I've promised you a ewe?

WIDOW QUIN. A ewe's a small thing, but what would you give me if I did wed him and did save you so?

SHAWN (*with astonishment*). You?

WIDOW QUIN. Aye. Would you give me the red cow you have and the mountainy ram, and the right of way across your rye path, and a load of dung at Michaelmas,[36] and turbary[37] upon the western hill?

SHAWN (*radiant with hope*). I would surely, and I'd give you the wedding-ring I have, and the loan of a new suit, the way you'd have him decent on the wedding-day. I'd give you two kids for your dinner, and a gallon of poteen, and I'd call the piper on the long car[38] to your wedding from Crossmolina[39] or from Ballina.[40] I'd give you . . .

WIDOW QUIN. That'll do, so, and let you whisht, for he's coming now again.

(CHRISTY *comes in very natty in the new clothes.* WIDOW QUIN *goes to him admiringly.*)

WIDOW QUIN. If you seen yourself now, I'm thinking you'd be too proud to speak to us at all, and it'd be a pity surely to have your like sailing from Mayo to the Western World.[41]

[33] **again him** against him   [34] **Kilmainham** once notorious Dublin jail   [35] **pike** pitchfork   [36] **Michaelmas** feast of St. Michael and All Angels, September 29th   [37] **turbary** right to cut turf (peat)   [38] **long car** an enlarged, four-wheeled, jaunting car   [39] **Crossmolina** a small market town of North-East Mayo   [40] **Ballina** market town and small seaport of North Mayo   [41] **Western World** America

CHRISTY (*as proud as a peacock*). I'm not going. If this is a poor place itself, I'll make myself contented to be lodging here.

(WIDOW QUIN *makes a sign to* SHAWN *to leave them.*)

SHAWN. Well, I'm going measuring the racecourse while the tide is low, so I'll leave you the garments and my blessing for the sports to-day. God bless you!
(*He wriggles out.*)

WIDOW QUIN (*admiring* CHRISTY). Well, you're mighty spruce, young fellow. Sit down now while you're quiet till you talk with me.

CHRISTY (*swaggering*). I'm going abroad on the hill-side for to seek Pegeen.

WIDOW QUIN. You'll have time and plenty for to seek Pegeen, and you heard me saying at the fall of night the two of us should be great company.

CHRISTY. From this out I'll have no want of company when all sorts is bringing me their food and clothing (*he swaggers to the door, tightening his belt*), the way they'd set their eyes upon a gallant orphan cleft his father with one blow to the breeches belt. (*He opens door, then staggers back.*) Saints of glory! Holy angels from the throne of light!

WIDOW QUIN (*going over*). What ails you?

CHRISTY. It's the walking spirit of my murdered da!

WIDOW QUIN (*looking out*). Is it that tramper?

CHRISTY (*wildly*). Where'll I hide my poor body from that ghost of hell?

(*The door is pushed open, and* OLD MAHON *appears on threshold.* CHRISTY *darts in behind door.*)

WIDOW QUIN (*in great amusement*). God save you, my poor man.

MAHON (*gruffly*). Did you see a young lad passing this way in the early morning or the fall of night?

WIDOW QUIN. You're a queer kind to walk in not saluting at all.

MAHON. Did you see the young lad?

WIDOW QUIN (*stiffly*). What kind was he?

MAHON. An ugly young streeler[42] with a murderous gob[43] on him, and a little switch in his hand. I met a tramper seen him coming this way at the fall of night.

WIDOW QUIN. There's harvest hundreds do be passing these days for the Sligo[44] boat. For what is it you're wanting him, my poor man?

MAHON. I want to destroy him for breaking the head on me with the clout of a loy. (*He takes off a big hat, and shows his head in a mass of bandages and plaster, with some pride.*) It was he did that, and amn't I a great wonder to think I've traced him ten days with that rent in my crown?

WIDOW QUIN (*taking his head in both hands and examining it with extreme delight*). That was a great blow. And who hit you? A robber maybe?

MAHON. It was my own son hit me, and he the divil a robber, or anything else, but a dirty, stuttering lout.

WIDOW QUIN (*letting go his skull and wiping her hands in her apron*). You'd best be wary of a mortified scalp, I think they call it, lepping around with that wound in the splendour of the sun. It was a bad blow surely, and you should have vexed him fearful to make him strike that gash in his da.

MAHON. Is it me?

WIDOW QUIN (*amusing herself*). Aye. And isn't it a great shame when the old and hardened do torment the young?

MAHON (*raging*). Torment him is it? And I after holding out with the patience of a martyred saint till there's nothing but destruction on, and I'm driven out in my old age with none to aid me.

WIDOW QUIN (*greatly amused*). It's a sacred wonder the way that wickedness will spoil a man.

---

[42] **streeler** an idle, slovenly person   [43] **gob** mouth   [44] **Sligo** large town and seaport north of Mayo. Seasonal migrants sailed from Sligo for Scotland and England to seek work as harvesters and, with their meagre earnings, to return to pay the rents on their tiny holdings

MAHON. My wickedness, is it? Amn't I after saying it is himself has me destroyed, and he a liar on walls,[45] a talker of folly, a man you'd see stretched the half of the day in the brown ferns with his belly to the sun.

WIDOW QUIN. Not working at all?

MAHON. The divil a work, or if he did itself, you'd see him raising up a haystack like the stalk of a rush, or driving our last cow till he broke her leg at the hip, and when he wasn't at that he'd be fooling over little birds he had—finches and felts[46]—or making mugs at his own self in the bit of a glass we had hung on the wall.

WIDOW QUIN (*looking at* CHRISTY). What way was he so foolish? It was running wild after the girls maybe?

MAHON (*with a shout of derision*). Running wild, is it? If he seen a red petticoat coming swinging over the hill, he'd be off to hide in the sticks, and you'd see him shooting out his sheep's eyes between the little twigs and the leaves, and his two ears rising like a hare looking out through a gap. Girls, indeed!

WIDOW QUIN. It was drink maybe?

MAHON. And he a poor fellow would get drunk on the smell of a pint. He'd a queer rotten stomach, I'm telling you, and when I gave him three pulls from my pipe a while since, he was taken with contortions till I had to send him in the ass cart to the females' nurse.

WIDOW QUIN (*clasping her hands*). Well, I never till this day heard tell of a man the like of that!

MAHON. I'd take a mighty oath you didn't surely, and wasn't he the laughing joke of every female woman where four baronies meet, the way the girls would stop their weeding if they seen him coming the road to let a roar at him, and call him the looney[47] of Mahon's.

---

[45] **liar on walls** perhaps of the gossiping and boasting of men leaning against field walls [46] **felts** fieldfares [47] **looney** idle, stupid fellow

WIDOW QUIN. I'd give the world and all to see the like of him. What kind was he?

MAHON. A small low fellow.

WIDOW QUIN. And dark?

MAHON. Dark and dirty.

WIDOW QUIN (*considering*). I'm thinking I seen him.

MAHON (*eagerly*). An ugly young blackguard.[48]

WIDOW QUIN. A hideous, fearful villain, and the spit of you.

MAHON. What way is he fled?

WIDOW QUIN. Gone over the hills to catch a coasting steamer to the north or south.

MAHON. Could I pull up on him now?

WIDOW QUIN. If you'll cross the sands below where the tide is out, you'll be in it as soon as himself, for he had to go round ten miles by the top of the bay. (*She points to the door.*) Strike down by the head beyond and then follow on the roadway to the north and east.

(MAHON *goes abruptly.*)

WIDOW QUIN (*shouting after him*). Let you give him a good vengeance when you come up with him, but don't put yourself in the power of the law, for it'd be a poor thing to see a judge in his black cap reading out his sentence on a civil warrior the like of you.

(*She swings the door to and looks at* CHRISTY, *who is cowering in terror, for a moment, then she bursts into a laugh.*)

WIDOW QUIN. Well, you're the walking playboy of the western world, and that's the poor man you had divided to his breeches belt.

CHRISTY (*looking out: then, to her*). What'll Pegeen say when she hears that story? What'll she be saying to me now?

WIDOW QUIN. She'll knock the head of you, I'm thinking, and drive you from the door. God help her

[48] **blackguard** a scoundrel

to be taking you for a wonder, and you a little schemer making up a story you destroyed your da.

CHRISTY (*turning to the door, nearly speechless with rage, half to himself*). To be letting on he was dead, and coming back to his life, and following after me like an old weasel tracing a rat, and coming in here laying desolation between my own self and the fine women of Ireland, and he a kind of carcase that you'd fling upon the sea.[49] . . .

WIDOW QUIN (*more soberly*). There's talking[50] for a man's one only son.

CHRISTY (*breaking out*). His one son, is it? May I meet him with one tooth and it aching, and one eye to be seeing seven and seventy divils in the twists of the road, and one old timber leg on him to limp into the scalding grave. (*Looking out*) There he is now crossing the strands, and that the Lord God would send a high wave to wash him from the world.

WIDOW QUIN (*scandalised*). Have you no shame? (*putting her hand on his shoulder and turning him round*) What ails you? Near crying, is it?

CHRISTY (*in despair and grief*). Amn't I after seeing the love-light of the star of knowledge[51] shining from her brow, and hearing words would put you thinking on the holy Brigid[52] speaking to the infant saints, and now she'll be turning again, and speaking hard words to me, like an old woman with a spavindy ass[53] she'd have, urging on a hill.

WIDOW QUIN. There's poetry talk for a girl you'd see itching and scratching, and she with a stale stink of poteen on her from selling in the shop.

CHRISTY (*impatiently*). It's her like is fitted to be

[49] carcase . . . sea dead sheep and cattle are pushed over the cliffs into the ocean   [50] There's talking ironically, that's a fine thing to be saying   [51] star of knowledge conventional Irish love-image   [52] Brigid St. Brigid, or Bride (*ca.* 451-525), Abbess of Kildare, and, after St. Patrick greatest and most venerated of Irish saints   [53] spavindy ass an ass lame with spavin, a disease of the hock

handling merchandise in the heavens above, and what'll I be doing now, I ask you, and I a kind of wonder was jilted by the heavens when a day was by.

(*There is a distant noise of girls' voices.* WIDOW QUIN *looks from window and comes to him, hurriedly.*)

WIDOW QUIN. You'll be doing like myself, I'm thinking, when I did destroy my man, for I'm above many's the day, odd times in great spirits, abroad in the sunshine, darning a stocking or stitching a shift, and odd times again looking out on the schooners, hookers,[54] trawlers is sailing the sea, and I thinking on the gallant hairy fellows are drifting beyond, and myself long years living alone.

CHRISTY (*interested*). You're like me, so.

WIDOW QUIN. I am your like, and it's for that I'm taking a fancy to you, and I with my little houseen above where there'd be myself to tend you, and none to ask were you a murderer or what at all.

CHRISTY. And what would I be doing if I left Pegeen?

WIDOW QUIN. I've nice jobs you could be doing, gathering shells to make a whitewash for our hut within, building up a little goose-house, or stretching a new skin on an old curragh[55] I have, and if my hut is far from all sides, it's there you'll meet the wisest old men, I tell you, at the corner of my wheel,[56] and it's there yourself and me will have great times whispering and hugging. . . .

VOICES (*outside, calling far away*). Christy! Christy Mahon! Christy!

CHRISTY. Is it Pegeen Mike?

WIDOW QUIN. It's the young girls, I'm thinking, com-

---

[54] **hookers** a one-masted fishing-smack   [55] **curragh** (or curagh) a light, open boat made of a frame-work of lath covered formerly with hide or leather but now with tarred canvas   [56] **wheel** spinning wheel

ing to bring you to the sports below, and what is it you'll have me to tell them now?

CHRISTY. Aid me for to win Pegeen. It's herself only that I'm seeking now. (WIDOW QUIN *gets up and goes to window*.) Aid me for to win her, and I'll be asking God to stretch a hand to you in the hour of death, and lead you short cuts through the Meadows of Ease, and up the floor of Heaven to the Footstool of the Virgin's Son.

WIDOW QUIN. There's praying!

VOICES (*nearer*). Christy! Christy Mahon!

CHRISTY (*with agitation*). They're coming. Will you swear to aid and save me for the love of Christ?

WIDOW QUIN (*looks at him for a moment*). If I aid you, will you swear to give me a right of way I want, and a mountainy ram, and a load of dung at Michaelmas, the time that you'll be master here?

CHRISTY. I will, by the elements and stars of night.

WIDOW QUIN. Then we'll not say a word of the old fellow, the way Pegeen won't know your story till the end of time.

CHRISTY. And if he chances to return again?

WIDOW QUIN. We'll swear he's a maniac and not your da. I could take an oath I seen him raving on the sands to-day. (GIRLS *run in*.)

SUSAN. Come on to the sports below. Pegeen says you're to come.

SARA TANSEY. The lepping's beginning, and we've a jockey's suit to fit upon you for the mule race on the sands below.

HONOR. Come on, will you?

CHRISTY. I will then if Pegeen's beyond.

SARA. She's in the boreen[57] making game of Shaneen Keogh.

CHRISTY. Then I'll be going to her now.

(*He runs out followed by the girls.*)

[57]boreen a narrow road, a lane

WIDOW QUIN. Well, if the worst comes in the end of all, it'll be great game to see there's none to pity him but a widow woman, the like of me, has buried her children and destroyed her man.

(*She goes out.*)

CURTAIN

Act III

SCENE: *As before. Later in the day.* JIMMY *comes in, slightly drunk.*

JIMMY (*calls*). Pegeen! (*Crosses to inner door*) Pegeen Mike! (*Comes back again into the room*) Pegeen! (PHILLY *comes in in the same state.*) (*To* PHILLY) Did you see herself?

PHILLY. I did not; but I sent Shawn Keogh with the ass cart for to bear him home. (*Trying cupboards which are locked*) Well, isn't he a nasty man to get into such staggers at a morning wake? and isn't herself the divil's daughter for locking, and she so fussy after that young gaffer,[1] you might take your death with drought and none to heed you?

JIMMY. It's little wonder she'd be fussy, and he after bringing bankrupt ruin on the roulette man, and the trick-o'-the-loop[2] man, and breaking the nose of the cockshot-man,[3] and winning all in the sports below, racing, lepping, dancing, and the Lord knows what! He's right luck, I'm telling you.

PHILLY. If he has, he'll be rightly hobbled[4] yet, and he not able to say ten words without making a brag of

---

[1] **gaffer** a young chap   [2] **trick-o'-the-loop** to guess the center loop in a little leather belt   [3] **cockshot-man** a man with his face blackened, except one cheek and eye, standing shots of a wooden ball behind a board with a large hole in the middle   [4] **hobbled** legs tied together like an animal

the way he killed his father, and the great blow he hit
with the loy.

JIMMY. A man can't hang by his own informing, and
his father should be rotten by now.

(OLD MAHON *passes window slowly.*)

PHILLY. Supposing a man's digging spuds in that
field with a long spade, and supposing he flings up
the two halves of that skull, what'll be said then in
the papers and the courts of law?

JIMMY. They'd say it was an old Dane,[5] maybe, was
drowned in the flood. (OLD MAHON *comes in and sits
down near door listening.*) Did you never hear tell of
the skulls they have in the city of Dublin, ranged out
like blue jugs in a cabin of Connaught?

PHILLY. And you believe that?

JIMMY (*pugnaciously*). Didn't a lad see them and
he after coming from harvesting in the Liverpool boat?
"They have them there," says he, "making a show of
the great people there was one time walking the
world. White skulls and black skulls and yellow
skulls, and some with full teeth, and some haven't
only but one."

PHILLY. It was no lie, maybe, for when I was a
young lad, there was a graveyard beyond the house
with the remnants of a man who had thighs as long
as your arm. He was a horrid man, I'm telling you,
and there was many a fine Sunday I'd put him together for fun, and he with shiny bones, you wouldn't
meet the like of these days in the cities of the world.

MAHON (*getting up*). You wouldn't is it? Lay your
eyes on that skull, and tell me where and when there
was another the like of it, is splintered only from the
blow of a loy.

PHILLY. Glory be to God! And who hit you at all?

MAHON (*triumphantly*). It was my own son hit me.
Would you believe that?

[5] **Dane** Vikings raided Irish coast from the 9th to the 12th
centuries

JIMMY. Well, there's wonders hidden in the heart of man!

PHILLY (*suspiciously*). And what way was it done?

MAHON (*wandering about the room*). I'm after walking hundreds and long scores of miles, winning clean beds and the fill of my belly four times in the day, and I doing nothing but telling stories of that naked truth. (*He comes to them a little aggressively.*) Give me a supeen and I'll tell you now.

(WIDOW QUIN *comes in and stands aghast behind him. He is facing* JIMMY *and* PHILLY, *who are on the left.*)

JIMMY. Ask herself beyond. She's the stuff hidden in her shawl.

WIDOW QUIN (*coming to* MAHON *quickly*). You here, is it? You didn't go far at all?

MAHON. I seen the coasting steamer passing, and I got a drought upon me and a cramping leg, so I said, "The divil go along with him," and turned again. (*Looking under her shawl*) And let you give me a supeen, for I'm destroyed travelling since Tuesday was a week.

WIDOW QUIN (*getting a glass, in a cajoling tone*). Sit down then by the fire and take your ease for a space. You've a right to be destroyed indeed, with your walking, and fighting, and facing the sun (*giving him poteen from a stone jar she has brought in*). There now is a drink for you, and may it be to your happiness and length of life.

MAHON (*taking glass greedily, and sitting down by fire*). God increase you!

WIDOW QUIN (*taking men to the right stealthily*). Do you know what? That man's raving from his wound to-day, for I met him a while since telling a rambling tale of a tinker had him destroyed. Then he heard of Christy's deed, and he up and says it was his son had cracked his skull. O isn't madness a fright, for he'll

go killing someone yet, and he thinking it's the man
has struck him so?

JIMMY (*entirely convinced*). It's a fright surely. I
knew a party was kicked in the head by a red mare,
and he went killing horses a great while, till he eat
the insides of a clock and died after.

PHILLY (*with suspicion*). Did he see Christy?

WIDOW QUIN. He didn't. (*With a warning gesture*)
Let you not be putting him in mind of him, or you'll
be likely summoned if there's murder done. (*Looking
round at Mahon*) Whisht! He's listening. Wait now
till you hear me taking him easy and unravelling all.
(*She goes to* Mahon.) And what way are you feeling,
mister? Are you in contentment now?

MAHON (*slightly emotional from his drink*). I'm
poorly only, for it's a hard story the way I'm left to-
day, when it was I did tend him from his hour of
birth, and he a dunce never reached his second book,
the way he'd come from school, many's the day, with
his legs lamed under him, and he blackened with his
beatings like a tinker's ass. It's a hard story, I'm saying, the way some do have their next and nighest
raising up a hand of murder on them, and some is
lonesome getting their death with lamentation in the
dead of night.

WIDOW QUIN (*not knowing what to say*). To hear
you talking so quiet, who'd know you were the same
fellow we seen pass to-day?

MAHON. I'm the same surely. The wrack and ruin of
threescore years; and it's a terror to live that length, I
tell you, and to have your sons going to the dogs
against you, and you wore out scolding them, and
skelping[6] them, and God knows what.

PHILLY (*to* JIMMY). He's not raving. (*To* WIDOW
QUIN) Will you ask him what kind was his son?

WIDOW QUIN (*to* MAHON, *with a peculiar look*).
Was your son that hit you a lad of one year and a

[6] **skelping** hitting

score maybe, a great hand at racing and lepping and licking the world?

MAHON (*turning on her with a roar of rage*). Didn't you hear me say he was the fool of men, the way from this out he'll know the orphan's lot with old and young making game of him and they swearing, raging, kicking at him like a mangy cur.

(*A great burst of cheering outside, some way off*)

MAHON (*putting his hands to his ears*). What in the name of God do they want roaring below?

WIDOW QUIN (*with the shade of a smile*). They're cheering a young lad, the champion playboy of the Western World.   (*More cheering*)

MAHON (*going to window*). It'd split my heart to hear them, and I with pulses in my brain-pan[7] for a week gone by. Is it racing they are?

JIMMY (*looking from door*). It is then. They are mounting him for the mule race will be run upon the sands. That's the playboy on the winkered[8] mule.

MAHON (*puzzled*). That lad, is it? If you said it was a fool he was, I'd have laid a mighty oath he was the likeness of my wandering son (*uneasily, putting his hand to his head*). Faith, I'm thinking I'll go walking for to view the race.

WIDOW QUIN (*stopping him, sharply*). You will not. You'd best take the road to Belmullet, and not be dilly-dallying in this place where there isn't a spot you could sleep.

PHILLY (*coming forward*). Don't mind her. Mount there on the bench and you'll have a view of the whole. They're hurrying before the tide will rise, and it'd be near over if you went down the pathway through the crags below.

MAHON (*mounts on bench*, WIDOW QUIN *beside him*). That's a right view again the edge of the sea. They're coming now from the point. He's leading. Who is he at all?

[7] **brain-pan** the skull   [8] **winkered** wearing blinkers

WIDOW QUIN. He's the champion of the world, I tell you, and there isn't a hap'orth[9] isn't falling lucky to his hands to-day.

PHILLY (*looking out, interested in the race*). Look at that. They're pressing him now.

JIMMY. He'll win it yet.

PHILLY. Take you time, Jimmy Farrell. It's too soon to say.

WIDOW QUIN (*shouting*). Watch him taking the gate. There's riding.

JIMMY (*cheering*). More power to the young lad!

MAHON. He's passing the third.

JIMMY. He'll lick them yet!

WIDOW QUIN. He'd lick them if he was running races with a score itself.

MAHON. Look at the mule he has, kicking the stars.

WIDOW QUIN. There was a lep! (*Catching hold of* MAHON *in her excitement*) He's fallen! He's mounted again! Faith, he's passing them all!

JIMMY. Look at him skelping her!

PHILLY. And the mountain girls hooshing[10] him on!

JIMMY. It's the last turn! The post's cleared for them now!

MAHON. Look at the narrow place. He'll be into the bogs! (*With a yell.*) Good rider! He's through it again!

JIMMY. He's neck and neck!

MAHON. Good boy[11] to him! Flames, but he's in!

(*Great cheering, in which all join*)

MAHON (*with hesitation*). What's that? They're raising him up. They're coming this way. (*With a roar of rage and astonishment*) It's Christy! by the stars of God! I'd know his way of spitting and he astride the moon.

(*He jumps down and makes a run for the door, but* WIDOW QUIN *catches him and pulls him back.*)

---

[9] **hap'orth** a halfpenny worth   [10] **hooshing** a cry used to scare or drive away fowls, pigs   [11] **Good boy** brave and tough

WIDOW QUIN. Stay quiet, will you? That's not your son. (*To* JIMMY) Stop him, or you'll get a month for the abetting of manslaughter and be fined as well.

JIMMY. I'll hold him.

MAHON (*struggling*). Let me out! Let me out, the lot of you! till I have my vengeance on his head today.

WIDOW QUIN (*shaking him, vehemently*). That's not your son. That's a man is going to make a marriage with the daughter of this house, a place with fine trade, with a licence, and with poteen too.

MAHON (*amazed*). That man marrying a decent and a moneyed[12] girl! Is it mad yous are? Is it in a crazy-house for females that I'm landed now?

WIDOW QUIN. It's mad yourself is with the blow upon your head. That lad is the wonder of the Western World.

MAHON. I seen it's my son.

WIDOW QUIN. You seen that you're mad. (*Cheering outside*) Do you hear them cheering him in the zig-zags of the road? Aren't you after saying that your son's a fool, and how would they be cheering a true idiot born?

MAHON (*getting distressed*). It's maybe out of reason[13] that that man's himself. (*Cheering again*) There's none surely will go cheering him. Oh, I'm raving with a madness that would fright the world! (*He sits down with his hand to his head.*) There was one time I seen ten scarlet divils letting on they'd cork my spirit in a gallon can; and one time I seen rats as big as badgers sucking the lifeblood from the butt of my lug;[14] but I never till this day confused that dribbling idiot with a likely man. I'm destroyed surely.

WIDOW QUIN. And who'd wonder when it's your brain-pan that is gaping now?

MAHON. Then the blight of the sacred drought upon

[12] **moneyed** publicans are usually wealthy   [13] **out of reason** mad to think   [14] **lug** ear

myself and him, for I never went mad to this day, and I not three weeks with the Limerick[15] girls drinking myself silly, and parlatic[16] from the dusk to dawn. (*To* WIDOW QUIN, *suddenly*) Is my visage astray?

WIDOW QUIN. It is then. You're a sniggering maniac, a child could see.

MAHON (*getting up more cheerfully*). Then I'd best be going to the union[17] beyond, and there'll be a welcome before me, I tell you (*with great pride*), and I a terrible and fearful case, the way that there I was one time, screeching in a straightened waistcoat, with seven doctors writing out my sayings in a printed book. Would you believe that?

WIDOW QUIN. If you're a wonder itself, you'd best be hasty, for them lads caught a maniac one time and pelted the poor creature till he ran out, raving and foaming, and was drowned in the sea.

MAHON (*with philosophy*). It's true mankind is the divil when your head's astray. Let me out now and I'll slip down the boreen, and not see them so.

WIDOW QUIN (*showing him out*). That's it. Run to the right, and not a one will see. (*He runs off.*)

PHILLY (*wisely*). You're at some gaming, Widow Quin; but I'll walk after him and give him his dinner and a time to rest, and I'll see then if he's raving or as sane as you.

WIDOW QUIN (*annoyed*). If you go near that lad, let you be wary of your head, I'm saying. Didn't you hear him telling he was crazed at times?

PHILLY. I heard him telling a power; and I'm thinking we'll have right sport, before night will fall.

(*He goes out.*)

JIMMY. Well, Philly's a conceited and foolish man. How could that madman have his senses and his brain-

---

[15] **Limerick** one of the six counties of Munster whose capital city, Limerick, is situated at the head of the Shannon estuary [16] **parlatic** paralytic [17] **union** poorhouse, a concomitant of Irish landlordism, used to give shelter to tramps, the destitute and the imbecile

pan slit? I'll go after them and see him turn on Philly now.

(*He goes;* WIDOW QUIN *hides poteen behind counter. Then hubbub outside*)

VOICES. There you are! Good jumper! Grand lepper! Darlint boy! He's the racer! Bear him on, will you!

(CHRISTY *comes in, in jockey's dress, with* PEGEEN MIKE, SARA, *and other girls, and men.*)

PEGEEN (*to crowd*). Go on now and don't destroy him and he drenching with sweat. Go along, I'm saying, and have your tug-of-warring till he's dried his skin.

CROWD. Here's his prizes! A bagpipes! A fiddle was played by a poet in the years gone by! A flat and three-thorned blackthorn[18] would lick the scholars out of Dublin town!

CHRISTY (*taking prizes from the men*). Thank you kindly, the lot of you. But you'd say it was little only I did this day if you'd seen me a while since striking my one single blow.

TOWN CRIER (*outside, ringing a bell*). Take notice, last event of this day! Tug-of-warring on the green below! Come on, the lot of you! Great achievements for all Mayo men!

PEGEEN. Go on, and leave him for to rest and dry. Go on, I tell you, for he'll do no more. (*She hustles crowd out;* WIDOW QUIN *following them.*)

MEN (*going*). Come on then. Good luck for the while!

PEGEEN (*radiantly, wiping his face with her shawl*). Well, you're the lad, and you'll have great times from this out when you could win that wealth of prizes, and you sweating in the heat of noon!

CHRISTY (*looking at her with delight*). I'll have great times if I win the crowning prize I'm seeking now, and

[18] **blackthorn** a shillelagh

that's your promise that you'll wed me in a fortnight, when our banns[19] is called.

PEGEEN (*backing away from him*). You've right daring to go ask me that, when all knows you'll be starting to some girl in your own townland, when your father's rotten in four months, or five.

CHRISTY (*indignantly*). Starting from you, is it? (*He follows her.*) I will not, then, and when the airs is warming in four months, or five, it's then yourself and me should be pacing Neifin[20] in the dews of night, the times sweet smells do be rising, and you'd see a little, shiny new moon, maybe, sinking on the hills.

PEGEEN (*looking at him playfully*). And it's that kind of a poacher's love you'd make, Christy Mahon, on the sides of Neifin, when the night is down?

CHRISTY. It's little you'll think if my love's a poacher's, or an earl's itself, when you'll feel my two hands stretched around you, and I squeezing kisses on your puckered lips, till I'd feel a kind of pity for the Lord God is all ages sitting lonesome in his golden chair.

PEGEEN. That'll be right fun, Christy Mahon, and any girl would walk her heart out before she'd meet a young man was your like for eloquence, or talk, at all.

CHRISTY (*encouraged*). Let you wait, to hear me talking, till we're astray in Erris,[21] when Good Friday's[22] by, drinking a sup from a well, and making mighty kisses with our wetted mouths, or gaming in a gap of sunshine, with yourself stretched back unto your necklace, in the flowers of the earth.

PEGEEN (*in a lower voice, moved by his tone*). I'd be nice so, is it?

CHRISTY (*with rapture*). If the mitred bishops seen you that time, they'd be the like of the holy prophets, I'm thinking, do be straining the bars of Paradise to lay eyes on the Lady Helen of Troy, and she abroad,

---

[19] **banns** public announcement in church of a proposed marriage
[20] **Neifin** Mount Nephin. Its name belongs to the popular Irish love song of Connaught "The Brow of Néfin" [21] **Erris** a barony of North-West Mayo [22] **Good Friday's** when spring has come

pacing back and forward, with a nosegay in her golden shawl.

PEGEEN (*with real tenderness*). And what is it I have, Christy Mahon, to make me fitting entertainment for the like of you, that has such poet's talking, and such bravery of heart?

CHRISTY (*in a low voice*). Isn't there the light of seven heavens in your heart alone, the way you'll be an angel's lamp to me from this out, and I abroad in the darkness, spearing salmons in the Owen, or the Carrowmore?[23]

PEGEEN. If I was your wife, I'd be along with you those nights, Christy Mahon, the way you'd see I was a great hand at coaxing bailiffs, or coining funny nicknames for the stars of night.

CHRISTY. You, is it? Taking your death in the hailstones, or in the fogs of dawn.

PEGEEN. Yourself and me would shelter easy in a narrow bush, (*with a qualm of dread*) but we're only talking, maybe, for this would be a poor, thatched place to hold a fine lad is the like of you.

CHRISTY (*putting his arm round her*). If I wasn't a good Christian, it's on my naked knees I'd be saying my prayers and paters[24] to every jackstraw you have roofing your head, and every stony pebble is paving the laneway to your door.

PEGEEN (*radiantly*). If that's the truth, I'll be burning candles[25] from this out to the miracles of God that have brought you from the south to-day, and I, with my gowns bought ready, the way that I can wed you, and not wait at all.

CHRISTY. It's miracles, and that's the truth. Me there toiling a long while, and walking a long while, not knowing at all I was drawing all times nearer to this holy day.

PEGEEN. And myself, a girl, was tempted often to go

[23] **Owen . . . Carrowmore** Owen River and Lough Carrowmore of North-West Mayo   [24] **paters** paternosters   [25] **burning candles** votive lights

sailing the seas till I'd marry a Jew-man, with ten kegs
of gold, and I not knowing at all there was the like
of you drawing nearer, like the stars of God.

CHRISTY. And to think I'm long years hearing women
talking that talk, to all bloody fools, and this the first
time I've heard the like of your voice talking sweetly
for my own delight.

PEGEEN. And to think it's me is talking sweetly,
Christy Mahon, and I the fright of seven townlands
for my biting tongue. Well, the heart's a wonder; and,
I'm thinking, there won't be our like in Mayo, for
gallant lovers, from this hour, to-day. (*Drunken singing is heard outside.*) There's my father coming from
the wake, and when he's had his sleep we'll tell him,
for he's peaceful then. (*They separate.*)

MICHAEL (*singing outside*)—

> The jailor and the turnkey
> They quickly ran us down,
> And brought us back as prisoners
> Once more to Cavan town.

(*He comes in supported by* SHAWN.)

> There we lay bewailing
> All in a prison bound. . . .

(*He sees* CHRISTY. *Goes and shakes him drunkenly
by the hand, while* PEGEEN *and* SHAWN *talk on the
left.*)

MICHAEL (*to* CHRISTY). The blessing of God and the
holy angels on your head, young fellow. I hear tell
you're after winning all in the sports below; and wasn't
it a shame I didn't bear you along with me to Kate
Cassidy's wake, a fine, stout lad, the like of you, for
you'd never see the match of it for flows of drink,
the way when we sunk her bones at noonday in her
narrow grave, there were five men, aye, and six men,
stretched out retching speechless on the holy stones.

CHRISTY (*uneasily, watching* PEGEEN). Is that the truth?

MICHAEL. It is then, and aren't you a louty[26] schemer to go burying your poor father unbeknownst[27] when you'd a right to throw him on the crupper[28] of a Kerry mule and drive him westwards, like holy Joseph[29] in the days gone by, the way we could have given him a decent burial, and not have him rotting beyond, and not a Christian drinking a smart drop to the glory of his soul?

CHRISTY (*gruffly*). It's well enough he's lying, for the likes of him.

MICHAEL (*slapping him on the back*). Well, aren't you a hardened slayer? It'll be a poor thing for the household man where you go sniffing for a female wife; and (*pointing to Shawn*) look beyond at that shy and decent Christian I have chosen for my daughter's hand, and I after getting the gilded dispensation this day for to wed them now.

CHRISTY. And you'll be wedding them this day, is it?

MICHAEL (*drawing himself up*). Aye. Are you thinking, if I'm drunk itself, I'd leave my daughter living single with a little frisky rascal is the like of you?

PEGEEN (*breaking away from* SHAWN). Is it the truth the dispensation's come?

MICHAEL (*triumphantly*). Father Reilly's after reading it in gallous[30] Latin, and "It's come in the nick of time," says he; "so I'll wed them in a hurry, dreading that young gaffer who'd capsize the stars."

PEGEEN (*fiercely*). He's missed his nick of time, for it's that lad, Christy Mahon, that I'm wedding now.

MICHAEL (*loudly with horror*). You'd be making him a son to me, and he wet and crusted with his father's blood?

PEGEEN. Aye. Wouldn't it be a bitter thing for a girl

---

[26] **louty** stupid [27] **unbeknownst** in secret [28] **crupper** rump [29] **Joseph** reference to the great and elaborate funeral Joseph gave to his father Jacob. *Genesis* L.1-14 [30] **gallous** fine

to go marrying the like of Shaneen, and he a middling kind of a scarecrow, with no savagery or fine words in him at all?

MICHAEL (*gasping and sinking on a chair*). Oh, aren't you a heathen daughter to go shaking the fat of my heart, and I swamped and drownded with the weight of drink? Would you have them turning on me the way that I'd be roaring to the dawn of day with the wind upon my heart? Have you not a word to aid me, Shaneen? Are you not jealous at all?

SHAWN (*in great misery*). I'd be afeard to be jealous of a man did slay his da.

PEGEEN. Well, it'd be a poor thing to go marrying your like. I'm seeing there's a world of peril for an orphan girl, and isn't it a great blessing I didn't wed you, before himself càme walking from the west or south?

SHAWN. It's a queer story you'd go picking a dirty tramp up from the highways of the world.

PEGEEN (*playfully*). And you think you're a likely beau to go straying along with, the shiny Sundays of the opening year, when it's sooner on a bullock's liver you'd put a poor girl thinking than on the lily or the rose?

SHAWN. And have you no mind of my weight of passion, and the holy dispensation, and the drift[31] of heifers I am giving, and the golden ring?

PEGEEN. I'm thinking you're too fine for the like of me, Shawn Keogh of Killakeen, and let you go off till you'd find a radiant lady with droves of bullocks on the plains of Meath,[32] and herself bedizened [33] in the diamond jewelleries of Pharaoh's ma. That'd be your match, Shaneen. So God save you now!

(*She retreats behind* CHRISTY.)

SHAWN. Won't you hear me telling you . . . ?

CHRISTY (*with ferocity*). Take yourself from this,

[31] **drift** herd [32] **Meath** County Meath in the midlands where the land is exceptionally fertile [33] **bedizened** dressed in vulgar finery

young fellow, or I'll maybe add a murder to my deeds to-day.

MICHAEL (*springing up with a shriek*). Murder is it? Is it mad yous are? Would you go making murder in this place, and it piled with poteen for our drink to-night? Go on to the foreshore if it's fighting you want, where the rising tide will wash all traces from the memory of man.

(*Pushing* SHAWN *towards* CHRISTY)

SHAWN (*shaking himself free, and getting behind* MICHAEL). I'll not fight him, Michael James. I'd liefer live a bachelor, simmering in passions to the end of time, than face a lepping savage the like of him has descended from the Lord knows where. Strike him yourself, Michael James, or you'll lose my drift of heifers and my blue bull from Sneem.

MICHAEL. Is it me fight him, when it's father-slaying he's bred to now? (*Pushing* SHAWN) Go on you fool and fight him now.

SHAWN (*coming forward a little*). Will I strike him with my hand?

MICHAEL. Take the loy is on your western side.

SHAWN. I'd be afeard of the gallows if I struck with that.

CHRISTY (*taking up the loy*). Then I'll make you face the gallows or quit off [34] from this.

(SHAWN *flies out of the door.*)

CHRISTY. Well, fine weather be after him, (*going to* MICHAEL, *coaxingly*) and I'm thinking you wouldn't wish to have that quaking blackguard in your house at all. Let you give us your blessing and hear her swear her faith to me, for I'm mounted on the spring-tide of the stars of luck, the way it'll be good for any to have me in the house.

PEGEEN (*at the other side of* MICHAEL). Bless us

[34] **quit off** get out

now, for I swear to God I'll wed him, and I'll not renege.

MICHAEL (*standing up in the centre, holding on to both of them*). It's the will of God, I'm thinking, that all should win an easy or a cruel end, and it's the will of God that all should rear up lengthy families for the nurture of the earth. What's a single man, I ask you, eating a bit in one house and drinking a sup in another, and he with no place of his own, like an old braying jackass strayed upon the rocks? (*To* CHRISTY) It's many would be in dread to bring your like into their house for to end them, maybe, with a sudden end; but I'm a decent man of Ireland, and I liefer face the grave untimely and I seeing a score of grandsons growing up little gallant swearers by the name of God, than go peopling my bedside with puny weeds the like of what you'd breed, I'm thinking, out of Shaneen Keogh. (*He joins their hands.*) A daring fellow is the jewel of the world, and a man did split his father's middle with a single clout, should have the bravery of ten, so may God and Mary and St. Patrick bless you, and increase you from this mortal day.

CHRISTY and PEGEEN. Amen, O Lord!

(*Hubbub outside*)

(OLD MAHON *rushes in, followed by all the crowd, and* WIDOW QUIN. *He makes a rush at* CHRISTY, *knocks him down, and begins to beat him.*)

PEGEEN (*dragging back his arm*). Stop that, will you? Who are you at all?

MAHON. His father, God forgive me!

PEGEEN (*drawing back*). Is it rose from the dead?

MAHON. Do you think I look so easy quenched with the tap of a loy? (*Beats* CHRISTY *again*)

PEGEEN (*glaring at* CHRISTY). And it's lies you told, letting on you had him slitted, and you nothing at all.

CHRISTY (*catching* MAHON's *stick*). He's not my father. He's a raving maniac would scare the world.

(*Pointing to* WIDOW QUIN) Herself knows it is true.

CROWD. You're fooling Pegeen! The Widow Quin seen him this day, and you likely knew! You're a liar!

CHRISTY (*dumbfounded*). It's himself was a liar, lying stretched out with an open head on him, letting on he was dead.

MAHON. Weren't you off racing the hills before I got my breath with the start I had seeing you turn on me at all?

PEGEEN. And to think of the coaxing glory we had given him, and he after doing nothing but hitting a soft blow and chasing northward in a sweat of fear. Quit off from this.

CHRISTY (*piteously*). You've seen my doings this day, and let you save me from the old man; for why would you be in such a scorch of haste to spur me to destruction now?

PEGEEN. It's there your treachery is spurring me, till I'm hard set to think you're the one I'm after lacing in my heart-strings half an hour gone by. (*To* MAHON) Take him on from this, for I think bad the world should see me raging for a Munster liar, and the fool of men.

MAHON. Rise up now to retribution, and come on with me.

CROWD (*jeeringly*). There's the playboy! There's the lad thought he'd rule the roost in Mayo. Slate[35] him now, mister.

CHRISTY (*getting up in shy terror*). What is it drives you to torment me here, when I'd asked the thunders of the might of God to blast me if I ever did hurt to any saving only that one single blow.

MAHON (*loudly*). If you didn't, you're a poor good-for-nothing, and isn't it by the like of you the sins of the whole world are committed?

CHRISTY (*raising his hands*). In the name of the Almighty God. . . .

MAHON. Leave troubling the Lord God. Would you

[35] slate thrash

have Him sending down droughts, and fevers, and the old hen[36] and the cholera morbus?[37]

CHRISTY (*to* WIDOW QUIN). Will you come between us and protect me now?

WIDOW QUIN. I've tried a lot, God help me, and my share is done.

CHRISTY (*looking round in desperation*). And I must go back into my torment is it, or run off like a vagabond straying through the Unions with the dusts of August making mudstains in the gullet of my throat, or the winds of March blowing on me till I'd take an oath I felt them making whistles of my ribs within?

SARA. Ask Pegeen to aid you. Her like does often change.

CHRISTY. I will not then, for there's torment in the splendour of her like, and she a girl any moon of midnight would take pride to meet, facing southwards on the heaths of Keel.[38] But what did I want crawling forward to scorch my understanding at her flaming brow?

PEGEEN (*to* MAHON, *vehemently, fearing she will break into tears*). Take him on from this or I'll set the young lads to destroy him here.

MAHON (*going to him, shaking his stick*). Come on now if you wouldn't have the company to see you skelped.

PEGEEN (*half laughing, through her tears*). That's it, now the world will see him pandied,[39] and he an ugly liar was playing off the hero, and the fright of men.

CHRISTY (*to* MAHON, *very sharply*). Leave me go!

CROWD. That's it. Now Christy. If them two set fighting, it will lick the world.

MAHON (*making a grab at* CHRISTY). Come here to me.

---

[36] **old hen** influenza [37] **cholera morbus** cholera plague [38] **Keel** village on Achill Island [39] **pandied** flogged on the extended palm with a cane or ruler, a punishment to schoolboys

CHRISTY (*more threateningly*). Leave me go, I'm saying.

MAHON. I will maybe, when your legs is limping, and your back is blue.

CROWD. Keep it up, the two of you. I'll back the old one. Now the playboy.

CHRISTY (*in low and intense voice*). Shut your yelling, for if you're after making a mighty man of me this day by the power of a lie, you're setting me now to think if it's a poor thing to be lonesome, it's worse maybe go mixing with the fools of earth.

(MAHON *makes a movement towards him.*)

CHRISTY (*almost shouting*). Keep off . . . lest I do show a blow unto the lot of you would set the guardian angels winking in the clouds above.

(*He swings round with a sudden rapid movement and picks up a loy.*)

CROWD (*half frightened, half amused*). He's going mad! Mind yourselves! Run from the idiot!

CHRISTY. If I am an idiot, I'm after hearing my voice this day saying words would raise the topknot[40] on a poet in a merchant's town.[41] I've won your racing, and your lepping, and . . .

MAHON. Shut your gullet and come on with me.

CHRISTY. I'm going, but I'll stretch you first.

(*He runs at* OLD MAHON *with the loy, chases him out of the door, followed by crowd and* WIDOW QUIN. *There is a great noise outside, then a yell, and dead silence for a moment.* CHRISTY *comes in, half dazed, and goes to fire.*)

WIDOW QUIN (*coming in, hurriedly, and going to*

[40] **topknot** pompon   [41] **merchant's town** poets gathered at fairs in merchant towns

him). They're turning again you. Come on, or you'll be hanged, indeed.

CHRISTY. I'm thinking, from this out, Pegeen'll be giving me praises, the same as in the hours gone by.

WIDOW QUIN (*impatiently*). Come by the back door. I'd think bad to have you stifled on the gallows tree.

CHRISTY (*indignantly*). I will not, then. What good'd be my lifetime, if I left Pegeen?

WIDOW QUIN. Come on, and you'll be no worse than you were last night; and you with a double murder this time to be telling to the girls.

CHRISTY. I'll not leave Pegeen Mike.

WIDOW QUIN (*impatiently*). Isn't there the match of her in every parish public,[42] from Binghamstown[43] unto the plain of Meath? Come on, I tell you, and I'll find you finer sweethearts at each waning moon.

CHRISTY. It's Pegeen I'm seeking only, and what'd I care if you brought me a drift of chosen females, standing in their shifts itself, maybe, from this place to the Eastern World?

SARA (*runs in, pulling off one of her petticoats*). They're going to hang him. (*Holding out petticoat and shawl*) Fit these upon him, and let him run off to the east.

WIDOW QUIN. He's raving now; but we'll fit them on him, and I'll take him, in the ferry, to the Achill[44] boat.

CHRISTY (*struggling feebly*). Leave me go, will you? when I'm thinking of my luck to-day, for she will wed me surely, and I a proven hero in the end of all. (*They try to fasten petticoat round him.*)

WIDOW QUIN. Take his left hand, and we'll pull him now. Come on, young fellow.

CHRISTY (*suddenly starting up*). You'll be taking me from her? You're jealous, is it, of her wedding me? Go on from this.

[42] parish public public-house   [43] Binghamston a village on the Mullet   [44] Achill large island on the Mayo coast

(*He snatches up a stool, and threatens them with it.*)

WIDOW QUIN (*going*). It's in the madhouse they should put him, not in jail, at all. We'll go by the back door, to call the doctor, and we'll save him so.

(*She goes out, with* SARA, *through inner room. Men crowd in the doorway.* CHRISTY *sits down again by the fire.*)

MICHAEL (*in a terrified whisper*). Is the old lad killed surely?

PHILLY. I'm after feeling the last gasps quitting his heart.

(*They peer in at* CHRISTY.)

MICHAEL (*with a rope*). Look at the way he is. Twist a hangman's knot on it, and slip it over his head, while he's not minding at all.

PHILLY. Let you take it, Shaneen. You're the soberest of all that's here.

SHAWN. Is it me to go near him, and he the wickedest and worst with me? Let you take it, Pegeen Mike.

PEGEEN. Come on, so.

(*She goes forward with the others, and they drop the double hitch over his head.*)

CHRISTY. What ails you?

SHAWN (*triumphantly, as they pull the rope tight on his arms*). Come on to the peelers, till they stretch you now.

CHRISTY. Me!

MICHAEL. If we took pity on you, the Lord God would, maybe, bring us ruin from the law[45] to-day, so you'd best come easy, for hanging is an easy and a speedy end.

CHRISTY. I'll not stir. (*To* PEGEEN) And what is it

[45] **ruin . . . law** because of the poteen

you'll say to me, and I after doing it this time in the face of all?

PEGEEN. I'll say, a strange man is a marvel, with his mighty talk; but what's a squabble in your back yard, and the blow of a loy, have taught me that there's a great gap between a gallous story and a dirty deed. (*To men*) Take him on from this, or the lot of us will be likely put on trial for his deed to-day.

CHRISTY (*with horror in his voice*). And it's yourself will send me off, to have a horny-fingered hangman hitching his bloody slip-knots at the butt of my ear.

MEN (*pulling rope*). Come on, will you?

(*He is pulled down on the floor.*)

CHRISTY (*twisting his legs round the table*). Cut the rope, Pegeen, and I'll quit the lot of you, and live from this out, like the madmen[46] of Keel, eating muck and green weeds, on the faces of the cliffs.

PEGEEN. And leave us to hang, is it, for a saucy liar, the like of you? (*To men*) Take him on, out from this.

SHAWN. Pull a twist on his neck, and squeeze him so.

PHILLY. Twist yourself. Sure he cannot hurt you, if you keep your distance from his teeth alone.

SHAWN. I'm afeard of him (*To* PEGEEN) Lift a lighted sod, will you, and scorch his leg.

PEGEEN (*blowing the fire with a bellows*). Leave go now, young fellow, or I'll scorch your shins.

CHRISTY. You're blowing for to torture me? (*His voice rising and growing stronger*) That's your kind, is it? Then let the lot of you be wary, for, if I've to face the gallows, I'll have a gay march down, I tell you, and shed the blood of some of you before I die.

SHAWN (*in terror*). Keep a good hold, Philly. Be

[46] **madmen** gone mad from hunger in the famine days

wary, for the love of God. For I'm thinking he would liefest[47] wreak his pains on me.

CHRISTY (*almost gaily*). If I do lay my hands on you, it's the way you'll be at the fall of night, hanging as a scarecrow for the fowls of hell. Ah, you'll have a gallous jaunt I'm saying, coaching out through Limbo with my father's ghost.

SHAWN (*to* PEGEEN). Make haste, will you? Oh, isn't he a holy terror, and isn't it true for Father Reilly, that all drink's a curse that has the lot of you so shaky and uncertain now?

CHRISTY. If I can wring a neck among you, I'll have a royal judgment looking on the trembling jury in the courts of law. And won't there be crying out in Mayo the day I'm stretched upon the rope with ladies in their silks and satins snivelling in their lacy kerchiefs, and they rhyming songs and ballads on the terror of my fate?

(*He squirms round on the floor and bites* SHAWN'S *leg.*)

SHAWN (*shrieking*). My leg's bit on me. He's the like of a mad dog, I'm thinking, the way that I will surely die.

CHRISTY (*delighted with himself*). You will then, the way you can shake out hell's flags of welcome for my coming in two weeks or three, for I'm thinking Satan hasn't many have killed their da in Kerry, and in Mayo too. (OLD MAHON *comes in behind on all fours and looks on unnoticed.*)

MEN (*to* PEGEEN). Bring the sod, will you?

PEGEEN (*coming over*). God help him so. (*Burns his leg*)

CHRISTY (*kicking and screaming*). O, glory be to God!

(*He kicks loose from the table, and they all drag him towards the door.*)

[47] **liefest** most willingly

JIMMY (*seeing* OLD MAHON). Will you look what's come in?

(*They all drop* CHRISTY *and run left.*)

CHRISTY (*scrambling on his knees face to face with* OLD MAHON). Are you coming to be killed a third time, or what ails you now?

MAHON. For what is it they have you tied?

CHRISTY. They're taking me to the peelers to have me hanged for slaying you.

MICHAEL (*apologetically*). It is the will of God that all should guard their little cabins from the treachery of law, and what would my daughter be doing if I was ruined or was hanged itself?

MAHON (*grimly, loosening* CHRISTY). It's little I care if you put a bag on her back, and went picking cockles till the hour of death; but my son and myself will be going our own way, and we'll have great times from this out telling stories of the villainy of Mayo, and the fools is here. (*To* CHRISTY, *who is freed*) Come on now.

CHRISTY. Go with you, is it? I will then, like a gallant captain with his heathen slave. Go on now and I'll see you from this day stewing my oatmeal and washing my spuds, for I'm master of all fights from now. (*Pushing* MAHON) Go on, I'm saying.

MAHON. Is it me?

CHRISTY. Not a word out of you. Go on from this.

MAHON (*walking out and looking back at* CHRISTY *over his shoulder*). Glory be to God! (*With a broad smile*) I am crazy again! (*Goes*)

CHRISTY. Ten thousand blessings upon all that's here, for you've turned me a likely gaffer in the end of all, the way I'll go romancing through a romping lifetime from this hour to the dawning of the judgment day. (*He goes out.*)

MICHAEL. By the will of God, we'll have peace now for our drinks. Will you draw the porter, Pegeen?

SHAWN (*going up to her*). It's a miracle Father

Reilly can wed us in the end of all, and we'll have none to trouble us when his vicious bite is healed.

PEGEEN (*hitting him a box on the ear*). Quit my sight. (*Putting her shawl over her head and breaking out into wild lamentations*) Oh my grief, I've lost him surely. I've lost the only playboy of the Western World.

CURTAIN

RIDERS TO THE SEA

❧

A Play in One Act

INTRODUCTION

Between the silent cliffs of Clare and the Connemara coast are the Aran Islands, scene of *Riders to the Sea*. The play takes its title from a dramatic feature of life on the two small islands of Inishmaan and Inisheer. Because of the tides and shallows, coastal steamers and sometimes even smaller transports awaiting passengers and livestock must anchor far offshore. Consequently, islanders intent on shipping horses and cattle to the mainland must ride them into the sea and with the help of the agile island rowboats, the curaghs, tow the animals through the treacherous currents out to the steamer. In a sea that is seldom calm it is a hazardous business for man and beast. At the back of the curagh sits an island man who tethers the swimming animal until it is at the point of exhaustion. Then with a quick movement he pulls the beast's head over the gunnel and struggles to keep it alive and floating until it is hoisted aboard the steamer. This is one of the unique aspects of island life so powerfully captured in Robert Flaherty's splendid documentary film *Man of Aran* (1934).

Life on Aran has changed little from what it was when, at Yeats' uninspired recommendation, J. M. Synge went to the islands in 1898. There, in what he later called "The Last Fortress of the Celt," Synge found the raw material for most of his plays—the strange rhythms and rich imaginative language of his poetic speech, his artist's spirit and the soul of Ireland. He came upon a life that affected his simple, passionate heart—a life that was described in his prose work *The Aran Islands.* Later, Synge recollected his Aran experience in the peace of Wicklow and dramatized one tragic episode. First published in 1903, *Riders to the Sea* has been translated into at least eight languages and in 1937 was made into an opera by Vaughan Williams.

Riders is the story of one woman's struggle with the sea of life and death. To it she has already given her husband, his father, and five of her six sons. In the play, the sudden and almost simultaneous loss of her last two sons, Michael and Bartley, wrings from her tormented soul such a canticle of lament and resignation that it ennobles her grief. She becomes a symbol of the sorrowing mother of all mankind, death-taken in the unequal struggle. In her resignation she attains the heroic stature of an immortal, though captive, queen of the suffering.

Both the action and the characterization in *Riders to the Sea* are extraordinarily simple. In a sense, the action is over from the beginning. Everything is ready for burial; the chant alone must be sung, the prayers recited. Michael is dead, and Bartley, deaf to the sea's rage and to his mother Maurya's anguish, will be dead in a moment. Maurya alone awaits the alleviation of suffering. Of all the characters she shows progression. The sea is everywhere, inexorably the same despite her prayers and the young priest's trust in God. Bartley is drowned. Nora and Cathleen, still young, have yet to come to terms with the sea, while Maurya's motherhood has died in all her sons, their father and their grandfather. In her lament and resignation, universal grief finds prayer, patience, and peace. The end is inevitable, but there is a way to the inevitable that each soul must live out "if it's only a bit of wet flour we do have to eat, and maybe a fish that would be stinking." Pain is past. Life continues. The sea rushes on. "No man at all can be living for ever, and we must be satisfied."

Although the action is simple and the characterization slight, Synge achieves an art of a very high order. Through the native vigor of his speech, with its simplicity, dignity, and elemental rhythms, he captures the universal rhythms of life, death, and resignation. Through his functional imagery he suggests the omnipresent force of nature surrounding the island people, dwarfing their life efforts as they struggle against their inevitable fate. In domestic objects with their natural symbolism—bread, knife, rope, boards, shirt, and stockings—Synge compresses action and meaning to intensify climactic force. For example, he heightens the tragic implications of Bartley's being carried in "laid on a plank, with a bit of sail over it" by having this follow immediately Maurya's description of how Stephen and Shawn were brought home on a plank and how Patch was carried to her "in the half of a red sail, and water dripping out of it— . . ." Through Maurya's description Synge prepares the audience to anticipate the pathos in Bartley's return to her for requiem. Having brought his audience to sympathize with Maurya through the recital of past grief, Synge leads them to a confrontal of her present anguish. The paralysis of her confused recognition is followed by a sudden, cathartic contraction of her grief into an expansion of relief and resignation; she confesses, as though in a trance: "They're all gone now, and there isn't anything more the sea can do to me." Finally, with antiphonal dialogue, foreboding vision, elegies for the dead, and chant of the keen, Synge evokes the force of ancient ritual in this tragedy. The play's simplicity, dignity, and solemnity has more than once caused over-enthusiastic critics to exclaim with Yeats on hearing *Riders:* "Sophocles! No, Aeschylus!"

The history of the play's criticism, however, indicates that not all critics agree with Yeats' praise of *Riders;* James Joyce and others are troubled by the play's brevity. Still others, disturbed by the seeming lack of dramatic structure do not hesitate to call *Riders* a tone poem, a tragic idyl, almost a tragic epigram. On the other hand, many critics continue to acclaim *Riders* as the only true masterpiece of static drama, the greatest one-act tragedy in the modern theatre. The question of whether or not an Irish tragedy must conform to the Aristotelian standard has been a critics' dispute. However, *Riders to the Sea* continues to be theatrically effective. Its stark imagery, native rhythms, and intense pathos unite in an echo of the primordial cry for life as life itself is threatened with loss. The work shows that in the final resignation, heroic stature can enrich the spirit and grant it a timeless peace.

RIDERS TO THE SEA

PERSONS

MAURYA, *an old woman*
BARTLEY, *her son*
CATHLEEN, *her daughter*
NORA, *a younger daughter*
MEN and WOMEN

RIDERS TO THE SEA

SCENE: *An Island off the West of Ireland.*

(*Cottage kitchen, with nets, oilskins, spinning wheel, some new boards standing by the wall, etc.* CATHLEEN, *a girl of about twenty, finishes kneading cake, and puts it down in the pot-oven by the fire; then wipes her hands, and begins to spin at the wheel.* NORA, *a young girl, puts her head in at the door.*)

NORA (*in a low voice*). Where is she?

CATHLEEN. She's lying down, God help her, and maybe sleeping, if she's able.

(NORA *comes in softly, and takes a bundle from under her shawl.*)

CATHLEEN (*spinning the wheel rapidly*). What is it you have?

NORA. The young priest is after bringing[1] them. It's a shirt and a plain stocking were got off a drowned man in Donegal.[2]

(CATHLEEN *stops her wheel with a sudden movement, and leans out to listen.*)

NORA. We're to find out if it's Michael's they are, some time herself[3] will be down looking by the sea.

CATHLEEN. How would they be Michael's, Nora? How would he go the length of that way to the far north?

NORA. The young priest says he's known the like of it. "If it's Michael's they are," says he, "you can tell

[1] **after bringing** has just brought   [2] **Donegal** bay, seaport, and county more than a hundred miles north of Aran   [3] **herself** their mother Maurya, the woman of the house

85

herself he's got a clean burial[4] by the grace of God, and if they're not his, let no one say a word about them, for she'll be getting her death,"[5] says he, "with crying and lamenting."

(*The door which* NORA *half closed is blown open by a gust of wind.*)

CATHLEEN (*looking out anxiously*). Did you ask him would he stop Bartley going[6] this day with the horses to the Galway fair?[7]

NORA. "I won't stop him," says he, "but let you not be afraid. Herself does be saying prayers half through the night, and the Almighty God won't leave her destitute," says he, "with no son living."

CATHLEEN. Is the sea bad by the white rocks, Nora?

NORA. Middling bad, God help us. There's a great roaring in the west, and it's worse it'll be getting when the tide's turned to[8] the wind. (*She goes over to the table with the bundle.*) Shall I open it now?

CATHLEEN. Maybe she'd wake up on us, and come in before we'd done. (*Coming to the table*) It's a long time we'll be, and the two of us crying.

NORA (*goes to the inner door and listens*). She's moving about on the bed. She'll be coming in a minute.

CATHLEEN. Give me the ladder, and I'll put them up in the turf-loft, the way[9] she won't know of them at all, and maybe when the tide turns she'll be going down to see would he be floating from the east.

(*They put the ladder against the gable of the chimney;* CATHLEEN *goes up a few steps and hides the bundle in the turf-loft.* MAURYA *comes from the inner room.*)

---

[4] **clean burial** ritual burial   [5] **getting her death** Anglo-Irish idiom for *to die of*   [6] **going** from going   [7] **Galway fair** the natural mainland trade center for the islanders. Originally the phrase read "going this day to Connemara"   [8] **turned to** turned *against* to form a fierce sea   [9] **the way** so that

MAURYA (*looking up at* CATHLEEN *and speaking querulously*). Isn't it turf enough[10] you have for this day and evening?

CATHLEEN. There's a cake baking at the fire for a short space (*throwing down the turf*), and Bartley will want it when the tide turns if he goes to Connemara.[11]

(NORA *picks up the turf and puts it round the pot-oven.*)

MAURYA (*sitting down on a stool at the fire*). He won't go this day with the wind rising from the south and west. He won't go this day, for the young priest will stop him surely.

NORA. He'll not stop him, mother, and I heard Eamon Simon and Stephen Pheety and Colum Shawn saying he would go.

MAURYA. Where is he itself?

NORA. He went down to see would there be another boat sailing in the week, and I'm thinking it won't be long till he's here now, for the tide's turning at the green head, and the hooker's[12] tacking from the east.

CATHLEEN. I hear some one passing the big stones.

NORA (*looking out*). He's coming now, and he in a hurry.

BARTLEY (*comes in and looks round the room. Speaking sadly and quietly*). Where is the bit of new rope,[13] Cathleen, was bought in Connemara?

CATHLEEN (*coming down*). Give it to him, Nora; it's on a nail by the white boards. I hung it up this morning, for the pig with the black feet was eating it.

[10] **turf enough** there is no peat on the islands so each family at great expense must buy turf brought over in boatloads from Connemara   [11] **Connemara** the mountainous district of the Galway coast due north of Aran. In Synge's time all the horses from the island were taken by boat to Connemara to graze in the hills from June to September   [12] **hooker** a stout, one-masted fishing-smack used also to transport horses and cattle between the islands and the mainland   [13] **new rope** to make a halter so he can ride the horses down into the sea to meet the Galway boat

NORA (*giving him a rope*). Is that it, Bartley?

MAURYA. You'd do right to leave that rope, Bartley, hanging by the boards. (*Bartley takes the rope.*) It will be wanting[14] in this place, I'm telling you, if Michael is washed up to-morrow morning, or the next morning, or any morning in the week, for it's a deep grave we'll make him by the grace of God.

BARTLEY (*beginning to work with the rope*). I've no halter the way I can ride down on the mare, and I must go now quickly. This is the one boat going for two weeks or beyond it,[15] and the fair will be a good fair for horses I heard them saying below.

MAURYA. It's a hard thing[16] they'll be saying below if the body is washed up and there's no man in it[17] to make the coffin, and I after giving a big price for the finest white boards you'd find in Connemara.

(*She looks round at the boards.*)

BARTLEY. How would it be washed up, and we[18] after looking each day for nine days, and a strong wind blowing a while back from the west and south?

MAURYA. If it isn't found itself,[19] that wind is raising the sea, and there was a star up against the moon,[20] and it rising in the night. If it was a hundred horses, or a thousand horses you had itself, what is the price of a thousand horses against a son where there is one son only?

BARTLEY (*working at the halter, to* CATHLEEN). Let you go down each day, and see the sheep aren't jumping in on the rye, and if the jobber[21] comes you can sell the pig with the black feet if there is a good price going.

MAURYA. How would the like of her get a good price for a pig?

---

[14] **wanting** needed to lower coffin into grave [15] **beyond it** or more [16] **hard thing** bitter remarks [17] **in it** here in the house [18] **and we** when we're [19] **If . . . itself** even if [20] **star . . . moon** an omen in local folklore [21] **jobber** a livestock dealer

BARTLEY (*to* CATHLEEN). If the west wind holds with the last bit of the moon let you and Nora get up weed enough for another cock for the kelp.[22] It's hard set[23] we'll be from this day with no one in it[24] but one man to work.

MAURYA. It's hard set we'll be surely the day you're drownd'd with the rest. What way[25] will I live and the girls with me, and I an old woman looking for the grave?

(BARTLEY *lays down the halter, takes off his old coat, and puts on a newer one of the same flannel.*)

BARTLEY (*to* NORA). Is she coming to the pier?

NORA (*looking out*). She's passing the green head and letting fall her sails.

BARTLEY (*getting his purse and tobacco*). I'll have half an hour to go down, and you'll see me coming again in two days, or in three days, or maybe in four days if the wind is bad.

MAURYA (*turning round to the fire, and putting her shawl over her head*). Isn't it a hard and cruel man won't hear a word from an old woman, and she holding him from the sea?

CATHLEEN. It's the life of a young man to be going on the sea, and who would listen to an old woman with one thing and she saying it over?

BARTLEY (*taking the halter*). I must go now quickly. I'll ride down on the red mare, and the gray pony'll run behind me. . . . The blessing of God on you.

(*He goes out.*)

MAURYA (*crying out as he is in the door*). He's gone now, God spare us, and we'll not see him again. He's gone now, and when the black night is falling I'll have no son left me in the world.

---

[22] **weed . . . cock . . . kelp** seaweed heaped in a conical shaped mound, a rick, left to dry and then burned. The residue is left to harden and then sold for its iodine content   [23] **hard set** bad off   [24] **in it** here   [25] **What way** How

CATHLEEN. Why wouldn't you give him your blessing[26] and he looking round in the door? Isn't it sorrow enough is on every one in this house without your sending him out with an unlucky word behind him, and a hard word in his ear?

(MAURYA *takes up the tongs and begins raking the fire aimlessly without looking round.*)

NORA (*turning towards her*). You're taking away the turf from the cake.

CATHLEEN (*crying out*). The Son of God forgive us, Nora, we're after forgetting his bit of bread.

(*She comes over to the fire.*)

NORA. And it's destroyed[27] he'll be going till dark night, and he after eating nothing since the sun went up.

CATHLEEN (*turning the cake out of the oven*). It's destroyed he'll be, surely. There's no sense left on any person in a house where an old woman will be talking for ever.

(MAURYA *sways herself on her stool.*)

CATHLEEN (*cutting off some of the bread and rolling it in a cloth; to* MAURYA). Let you go down now to the spring well and give him this and he passing.[28] You'll see him then and the dark word will be broken, and you can say "God speed you," the way he'll be easy[29] in his mind.

MAURYA (*taking the bread*). Will I be in it[30] as soon as himself?

CATHLEEN. If you go now quickly.

MAURYA (*standing up unsteadily*). It's hard set I am to walk.

[26] blessing commonly considered bad luck not to return the blessing to one going off on a journey　[27] destroyed Anglo-Irish intensive for fatigued, exhausted　[28] and he passing when he's passing　[29] easy calm, tranquil　[30] in it there

CATHLEEN (*looking at her anxiously*). Give her the stick, Nora, or maybe she'll slip on the big stones.

NORA. What stick?

CATHLEEN. The stick Michael brought from Connemara.

MAURYA (*taking a stick NORA gives her*). In the big world the old people do be leaving things after them for their sons and children, but in this place it is the young men do be leaving things behind for them that do be old.

(*She goes out slowly. NORA goes over to the ladder.*)

CATHLEEN. Wait, Nora, maybe she'd turn back quickly. She's that sorry, God help her, you wouldn't know the thing she'd do.

NORA. Is she gone round by the bush?[31]

CATHLEEN (*looking out*). She's gone now. Throw it down quickly, for the Lord knows when she'll be out of it[32] again.

NORA (*getting the bundle from the loft*). The young priest said he'd be passing to-morrow, and we might go down and speak to him below if it's Michael's they are surely.

CATHLEEN (*taking the bundle*). Did he say what way they were found?

NORA (*coming down*). "There were two men," says he, "and they rowing round with poteen[33] before the cocks crowed, and the oar of one of them caught the body, and they passing the black cliffs[34] of the north."

CATHLEEN (*trying to open the bundle*). Give me a knife, Nora, the string's perished[35] with the salt water,

---

[31] **bush** an easy landmark on those treeless limestone wastes   [32] **out of it** out of the house   [33] **poteen** illicit whiskey   [34] **black cliffs** perhaps the stupendous cliffs of Slieve League rising nearly 2,000 feet out of the Atlantic on the north shore of Donegal Bay   [35] **perished** contracted and hardened

and there's a black knot[36] on it you wouldn't loosen in a week.

NORA (*giving her a knife*). I've heard tell it was a long way to Donegal.

CATHLEEN (*cutting the string*). It is surely. There was a man here a while ago—the man sold us that knife—and he said if you set off walking from the rocks beyond, it would be in seven days you'd be in Donegal.

NORA. And what time would a man take, and he floating?

(CATHLEEN *opens the bundle and takes out a bit of a stocking. They look at them eagerly.*)

CATHLEEN (*in a low voice*). The Lord spare us, Nora! isn't it a queer hard thing to say if it's his they are surely?

NORA. I'll get his shirt off the hook the way[37] we can put the one flannel on the other. (*She looks through some clothes hanging in the corner.*) It's not with them, Cathleen, and where will it be?

CATHLEEN. I'm thinking Bartley put it on him in the morning, for his own shirt was heavy with the salt in it (*pointing to the corner*). There's a bit of a sleeve was of the same stuff. Give me that and it will do. (NORA *brings it to her and they compare the flannel.*)

CATHLEEN. It's the same stuff, Nora; but if it is itself[38] aren't there great rolls of it in the shops of Galway, and isn't it many another man may have a shirt of it as well as Michael himself?

NORA (*who has taken up the stocking and counted the stitches, crying out*). It's Michael, Cathleen, it's Michael; God spare his soul, and what will herself[39] say when she hears this story, and Bartley on the sea?

CATHLEEN (*taking the stocking*). It's a plain stocking.

[36] black knot exceedingly hard to undo   [37] the way so that
[38] if it is itself even if it is   [39] herself Maurya

NORA. It's the second one of the third pair I knitted, and I put up three score stitches, and I dropped four of them.

CATHLEEN (*counts the stitches*). It's that number is in it (*crying out*). Ah, Nora, isn't it a bitter thing to think of him floating that way to the far north, and no one to keen[40] him but the black hags[41] that do be flying on the sea?

NORA (*swinging herself half round, and throwing out her arms on the clothes*). And isn't it a pitiful thing when there is nothing left of a man who was a great rower and fisher, but a bit of an old shirt and a plain stocking?

CATHLEEN (*after an instant*). Tell me is herself coming, Nora? I hear a little sound on the path.

NORA (*looking out*). She is, Cathleen. She's coming up to the door.

CATHLEEN. Put these things away before she'll come in. Maybe it's easier she'll be after giving her blessing to Bartley, and we won't let on[42] we've heard anything the time he's on the sea.

NORA (*helping* CATHLEEN *tc close the bundle*). We'll put them here in the corner.

(*They put them into a hole in the chimney corner.* CATHLEEN *goes back to the spinning-wheel.*)

NORA. Will she see it was crying I was?

CATHLEEN. Keep your back to the door the way the light'll not be on you.

(NORA *sits down at the chimney corner, with her back to the door.* MAURYA *comes in very slowly, without looking at the girls, and goes over to her stool at the other side of the fire. The cloth with the bread is*

---

[40] **keen** the ritual "Irish cry" of lamentation for the dead. Though improvised to a degree, it has several traditional phrases for it, each with many repetitions of the words Och, Ochone (Woe, woe!). The words are more spoken than sung [41] **black hags** cormorants [42] **won't let on** pretend we haven't heard

still in her hand. The girls look at each other, and
NORA *points to the bundle of bread.*)

CATHLEEN (*after spinning for a moment*). You
didn't give him his bit of bread?

(MAURYA *begins to keen softly, without turning
round.*)

CATHLEEN. Did you see him riding down?

(MAURYA *goes on keening.*)

CATHLEEN (*a little impatiently*). God forgive you;
isn't it a better thing to raise your voice and tell what
you seen, than to be making lamentation for a thing
that's done? Did you see Bartley, I'm saying to you.

MAURYA (*with a weak voice*). My heart's broken
from this day.

CATHLEEN (*as before*). Did you see Bartley?

MAURYA. I seen the fearfulest thing.

CATHLEEN (*leaves her wheel and looks out*). God
forgive you; he's riding the mare now over the green
head, and the gray pony behind him.

MAURYA (*starts, so that her shawl falls back from
her head and shows her white tossed hair. With a
frightened voice*). The gray pony behind him. . . .

CATHLEEN (*coming to the fire*). What is it ails you,
at all?

MAURYA (*speaking very slowly*). I've seen the fearfulest thing any person has seen, since the day Bride
Dara seen the dead man with the child in his arms.

CATHLEEN AND NORA. Uah.

(*They crouch down in front of the old woman at
the fire.*)

NORA. Tell us what it is you seen.

MAURYA. I went down to the spring well, and I
stood there saying a prayer to myself. Then Bartley
came along, and he riding on the red mare with the

gray pony[43] behind him. (*She puts up her hands, as if to hide something from her eyes.*) The Son of God spare us, Nora!

CATHLEEN. What is it you seen?

MAURYA. I seen Michael himself.

CATHLEEN (*speaking softly*). You did not, mother. It wasn't Michael you seen, for his body is after being found in the far north, and he's got a clean burial by the grace of God.

MAURYA (*a little defiantly*). I'm after seeing him this day, and he riding and galloping. Bartley came first on the red mare; and I tried to say "God speed you," but something choked the words in my throat. He went by quickly; and "the blessing of God on you," says he, and I could say nothing, I looked up then, and I crying, at the gray pony, and there was Michael upon it—with fine clothes on him, and new shoes on his feet.

CATHLEEN (*begins to keen*). It's destroyed we are from this day. It's destroyed, surely.

NORA. Didn't the young priest say the Almighty God won't leave her destitute with no son living?

MAURYA (*in a low voice, but clearly*). It's little the like of him[44] knows of the sea. . . . Bartley will be lost now, and let you call in Eamon and make me a good coffin out of the white boards, for I won't live after them. I've had a husband, and a husband's father, and six sons in this house—six fine men, though it was a hard birth I had with every one of them and they coming to the world—and some of them were found and some of them were not found, but they're gone now the lot of them. . . . There were Stephen, and Shawn, were lost in the great wind, and found

---

[43] red mare . . . gray pony other than being the traditional ballad colors for life and death, red and gray are also the predominant colors of the island clothing   [44] like of him men who live by the sea and not by the Chapel alone know it's little the sea cares for God or man

after in the Bay of Gregory[45] of the Golden Mouth, and carried up the two of them on one plank, and in by that door.

(*She pauses for a moment, the girls start as if they heard something through the door that is half open behind them.*)

NORA (*in a whisper*). Did you hear that, Cathleen? Did you hear a noise in the north-east?

CATHLEEN (*in a whisper*). There's some one after crying out by the seashore.

MAURYA (*continues without hearing anything*). There was Sheamus and his father, and his own father again, were lost in a dark night, and not a stick or sign was seen of them when the sun went up. There was Patch after was drowned out of a curagh[46] that turned over. I was sitting here with Bartley, and he a baby, lying on my two knees, and I seen two women, and three women, and four women coming in, and they crossing themselves, and not saying a word. I looked out then, and there were men coming after them, and they holding a thing in the half of a red sail, and water dripping out of it—it was a dry day, Nora—and leaving a track to the door.

(*She pauses again with her hand stretched out towards the door. It opens softly and old women begin to come in, crossing themselves on the threshold, and kneeling down in front of the stage with their backs to the people, and the white waist-bands of the red petticoats they wear over their heads just seen from behind.*)

MAURYA (*half in a dream, to* CATHLEEN). Is it Patch, or Michael, or what is it at all?

CATHLEEN. Michael is after being found in the far

---

[45] **Bay of Gregory** Gregory Sound separates the island of Inishmore from Inishmaan   [46] **curagh** a very light, open boat made of a frame-work of lath covered with tarred canvas

north, and when he is found there how could he be here in this place?

MAURYA. There does be a power[47] of young men floating round in the sea, and what way would they know if it was Michael they had, or another man like him, for when a man is nine days in the sea, and the wind blowing, it's hard set his own mother would be to say what man was in it.[48]

CATHLEEN. It's Michael, God spare him, for they're after sending us a bit of his clothes from the far north.

(*She reaches out and hands* MAURYA *the clothes that belonged to Michael.* MAURYA *stands up slowly, and takes them in her hands.* NORA *looks out.*)

NORA. They're carrying a thing among them and there's water dripping out of it and leaving a track by the big stones.

CATHLEEN (*in a whisper to the women who have come in*). Is it Bartley it is?

ONE OF THE WOMEN. It is surely, God rest his soul.

(*Two younger women come in and pull out the table. Then men carry in the body of* BARTLEY, *laid on a plank, with a bit of a sail over it, and lay it on the table.*)

CATHLEEN (*to the women, as they are doing so*). What way was he drowned?

ONE OF THE WOMEN. The gray pony knocked him over into the sea, and he was washed out where there is a great surf on the white rocks.

(MAURYA *has gone over and knelt down at the head of the table. The women are keening softly and swaying themselves with a slow movement.* CATHLEEN *and* NORA *kneel at the other end of the table. The men kneel near the door.*)

[47] **a power** a large number   [48] **was in it** was there, who it was

MAURYA (*raising her head and speaking as if she did not see the people around her*). They're all gone now, and there isn't anything more the sea can do to me. . . . I'll have no call[49] now to be up crying and praying when the wind breaks from the south, and you can hear the surf is in the east, and the surf is in the west, making a great stir with the two noises, and they hitting one on the other. I'll have no call now to be going down and getting Holy Water[50] in the dark nights after Samhain,[51] and I won't care what way the sea is when the other women will be keening. (*To NORA*) Give me the Holy Water, Nora, there's a small sup still on the dresser.

(NORA *gives it to her.*)

MAURYA (*drops Michael's clothes across BARTLEY'S feet, and sprinkles the Holy Water over him*). It isn't that I haven't prayed for you, Bartley, to the Almighty God. It isn't that I haven't said prayers in the dark night till you wouldn't know what I'd be saying; but it's a great rest I'll have now, and it's time surely. It's a great rest I'll have now, and great sleeping in the long nights after Samhain, if it's only a bit of wet flour we do have to eat, and maybe a fish that would be stinking.

(*She kneels down again, crossing herself, and saying prayers under her breath.*)

CATHLEEN (*to an old man*). Maybe yourself and Eamon would make a coffin when the sun rises. We have fine white boards herself bought, God help her, thinking Michael would be found, and I have a new cake you can eat while you'll be working.

THE OLD MAN (*looking at the boards*). Are there nails with them?

[49] **no call** no need   [50] **Holy Water** water blessed for ritual use and commonly kept in Catholic homes for benediction and to ward off danger   [51] **Samhain** (pron. Sòw-in) All Souls Day, 1 November, the feast of the Dead and the old name for the beginning of winter

CATHLEEN. There are not, Colum; we didn't think of the nails.

ANOTHER MAN. It's a great wonder she wouldn't think of the nails, and all the coffins she's seen made already.

CATHLEEN. It's getting old she is, and broken.

(MAURYA *stands up again very slowly and spreads out the pieces of Michael's clothes beside the body, sprinkling them with the last of the Holy Water.*)

NORA (*in a whisper to* CATHLEEN). She's quiet now and easy; but the day Michael was drowned you could hear her crying out from this to the spring well. It's fonder she was of Michael, and would any one have thought that?

CATHLEEN (*slowly and clearly*). An old woman will be soon tired with anything she will do, and isn't it nine days herself is after crying and keening, and making great sorrow in the house?

MAURYA (*puts the empty cup mouth downwards on the table, and lays her hands together on* BARTLEY'S *feet*). They're all together this time, and the end is come. May the Almighty God have mercy on Bartley's soul, and on Michael's soul, and on the souls of Sheamus and Patch, and Stephen and Shawn (*bending her head*); and may He have mercy on my soul, Nora, and on the soul of every one is left living in the world.

(*She pauses, and the keen rises a little more loudly from the women, then sinks away.*)

MAURYA (*continuing*). Michael has a clean burial in the far north, by the grace of the Almighty God. Bartley will have a fine coffin out of the white boards, and a deep grave surely. What more can we want than that? No man at all can be living for ever, and we must be satisfied.

(*She kneels down again and the curtain falls slowly.*)

BIBLIOGRAPHY

EDITIONS

The Collected Works of J. M. Synge, 5 vols. (London, 1962—).
The Plays and Poems of J. M. Synge, ed. T. R. Henn (London, 1963).
The Works of John M. Synge, 4 vols. (Dublin, 1910).
The Works of John M. Synge, 4 vols. (London, 1932).

The Playboy of the Western World (Dublin, 1907).
Riders to the Sea (Dublin, 1903).

BIOGRAPHY

Bourgeois, Maurice, *John Millington Synge and the Irish Theatre* (London, 1913).
Greene, David H., and Edward M. Stephens, *J. M. Synge: 1871-1909* (New York, 1959).
O'Neill, M. J. "Holloway on Synge's Last Days," *Modern Drama* VI, No. 2 (Lawrence, Kansas, 1963).
Yeats, W. B., *Autobiographies* (London, 1955).
———, *Essays and Introductions* (New York, 1961).

CRITICISM and HISTORY

Boyd, E. A., *Ireland's Literary Renaissance* (New York, 1916).
Corkery, D., *Synge and Anglo-Irish Literature* (Cork, 1931).
Ellis-Fermor, Una, *The Irish Dramatic Movement* (London, 1939).
Fay, G., *The Abbey Theatre* (Dublin, 1958).

Fay, W. G., and C. Carswell, *The Fays of the Abbey Theatre* (New York, 1935).

Gregory, Lady Augusta, *Our Irish Theatre* (London, 1913).

Gwynn, S., *Irish Literature and Drama* (London, 1936).

Howarth, H., *The Irish Writers: 1880-1940* (New York, 1958).

Malone, A. E., *The Irish Drama* (New York, 1929).

Mercier, V., *The Irish Comic Tradition* (Oxford, 1962).

Price, A., *Synge and Anglo-Irish Drama* (London, 1961).

Robinson, L., *Ireland's Abbey Theatre, A History: 1899-1951* (London, 1951).

Yeats, W. B., *Explorations,* ed. Mrs. W. B. Yeats (New York, 1962).

RECORDINGS

Riders to the Sea and In the Shadow of the Glen, Radio Erin Production, Spoken Arts—743 (New Rochelle, N.Y.).

The Playboy of the Western World, Angel Album 3547-B, Cusack Productions (Dublin, 1955).

"The Songs of Aran," h Series, Folkways Ethı

WITHDRAWN